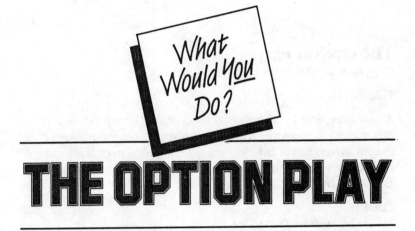

What Would You Do?

THE OPTION PLAY

By Bob Darden

Teenage
BOOKS

Group

Loveland, Colorado

The Option Play

Copyright © 1990 by Bob Darden

First Printing

Credits
Edited by Michael D. Warden
Cover designed by Judy Atwood Bienick
Interior designed by Judy Atwood Bienick
Cover illustration by Rand Kruback
Interior illustrations by Rand Kruback

Scripture quotations are from the Holy Bible, New International Version. Copyright © 1973, 1978, 1984 International Bible Society. Used by permission of Zondervan Bible Publishers.

Library of Congress Cataloging-in-Publication Data
Darden, Bob, 1954-
   The option play / by Bob Darden
     p.   cm.
   Summary: The reader helps junior Matt Brand make decisions about various aspects of high school sports including competition, popularity, steroids, success, failure and other issues.
   ISBN 1-55945-050-9
   1. Plot-your-own stories. [1. Football—Fiction. 2. High schools—Fiction. 3. Schools—Fiction. 4. Christian life—Fiction. 5. Plot-your-own stories.] I. Title.
PZ7.D24180p   1990
[Fic]—dc20   90-11041
                                CIP
                                AC

Printed in the United States of America

Dedication

To Steve Darden,
an athlete, a scholar, a gentleman
and a Christian example to his brother.

Acknowledgments

Thanks to Coaches Burris, Houston and Turner—three Christian men who taught me a lot about football and even more about the Christian faith.

Thanks to Jimmy King, an all-district quarterback who made all the right choices all the time.

And thanks to my beautiful wife, Mary, and the kids—Daniel, Rachel and Robert Van. We make a great team!

Your Road Map

The University of Texas Longhorns perfected the triple-option—or wishbone—offense. With each play, the quarterback has the option of handing off the football, keeping it or pitching it to a running back. The quarterback or any of the running backs can go up the middle, off-tackle or around the end on every play.

Sometimes the quarterback won't know where he's going to run until the play unfolds. And sometimes he won't make his decision until the last possible second, taking a hit just after pitching the ball back to the trailing running back.

Life's a lot like that. Each decision you make has several possible results. And sometimes you have several decisions to make in a single heartbeat.

The outcome of those decisions can be trivial—or life-changing.

That's how *The Option Play* is set up. Like real life, you make the decisions. You live with the consequences. At the end of each section you come to a moment of decision for Matt Brand, the main character. You make the choice for Matt—and yourself.

But here's a word of warning. Think twice before making any decision. One choice might be good for the moment, but bad in the long run. Another choice might appear to be the right thing to do—but for all the wrong reasons. Sometimes the choices are between what's good and what's better for Matt. And some decisions will result in events that are out of Matt's control. Sound a lot like your life? You bet!

In the end, Matt's just a normal guy. He messes up, he does well and he spends a lot of time doing stuff that's somewhere in between. You probably do too.

And who knows? Through all these decisions, maybe you'll learn an important truth right along with Matt. Want a hint? Okay—it doesn't matter if you're an all-state quarterback or a benchwarmer with the chess club, there's somebody who cares about you just as you are right now, somebody who loves you regardless. Somebody who'll always guide you to make the best choices for you.

Jesus—the ultimate "right choice."

The Option Play

Matt Brand hunched over the center, sweat trickling down the inside of his helmet. The Texas sun pounded his back.

He shouted hoarsely at his linemen. "Blue 28! Blue 28!"

The first-team linebackers leered at him across the line of scrimmage. Piece of cake.

"Hut! Hut!" Long pause. "Hut!"

The starters rushed through the second-team linemen in a wave. Matt barely had time to tuck the football into his gut before he was smothered with bodies.

Under the pile of bodies, Matt caught a glimpse of Martin Garcia, his best friend and woefully undersized 158-pound center. Martin was flat on his back.

"Yo, Martin. Must be 100 degrees in the shade down here."

Martin's grunt passed for a weak laugh. After the last player got off him, Martin rose heavily to his feet and signaled for the huddle.

Matt risked a glance at the sidelines. Coach Bob Charles was watching impassively, his clipboard clutched to his chest. This was the last day of two-a-day practices, the last chance to impress Coach, the last chance to make the varsity.

"Hey, Matt. Got an idea," Martin wheezed through his facemask. "Draw play. They're in the backfield before you are anyway. Use their speed against them. They'll overrun you."

"Good idea, guy. Nothin' else's worked—they're just teeing off on us." Matt turned to his fullback. "Dallas #2, fullback draw, between left tackle and guard. On 'Hut Hut.' Got it? Last chance, girls."

Matt led the battered second teamers to the line.

Coach isn't watching me, he's watching the A-team, Matt thought bitterly. Please, Lord, just let him look this way this once. Just one time give me a break, okay?

"Hut! Hut!"

The defensive line surged forward. Matt sprinted back as if to pass. A heartbeat before the giant nose tackle arrived, he handed off to his fullback. The nose tackle's helmet caught Matt square in the sternum, and he went down hard. The fullback slipped through the rush and lumbered 12 yards before the safety knocked him out of bounds near Coach Charles. Matt didn't see any of it. He was too busy wondering why the stars were out so early on a late Texas afternoon.

Coach stood stone-faced a moment before turning to Sammy Cruz, the fullback. "Good run, son." Then he walked out to the first-team defense. He grabbed James Lively, the middle linebacker, by the facemask.

"Boy, I've told you and *told* you to watch for the draw. Listen to me now! Where was your head? You thinking about that Salat girl, ain'cha? Well, that ain't gonna cut it with Kirbyville! Ten 'stands.' That goes for the rest of you on defense. Move it!" His whistle pierced the humid air.

James shot a venomous glance in Matt's direction, then stormed toward the bleachers. "Stands" was the most hated exercise of all. Ten times up and down the grandstands usually meant barked shins, skinned ankles and at least one fall.

When the first-team defense finished trudging up and down the bleachers, Coach Charles called everyone together.

"The coaches and I are posting the roster tomorrow morning here at the field house," he said flatly. "If your name isn't on the list, you're on the junior varsity under Coach Mills." Mills nodded his head in acknowledgment. "We'll issue the rest of your gear and uniforms tomorrow after school. Any questions?"

Silence.

"Oh, and one other thing," Coach drawled. "Don't come messin' around the field house before 8:00 in the morning. We're not posting the roster 'til then, and I don't want none of you numbskulls getting into trouble."

The boys talked among themselves as they walked back to the field house. Just before they arrived, Coach Charles turned and yanked a thumb toward Matt, Martin and some guys walking near the rear of the pack.

"You over there. You boys run back and pick up the rest of the gear from the practice fields and bring it in. Pronto."

"He doesn't even know my name," Matt complained to Martin. " 'You over there.' I haven't got a chance to make the squad." He kicked at a clump of grass.

"Oh, I dunno Matt," Martin said, tugging at a duffel bag full of footballs. "You've looked as good, if not better, than Ky. He's the only other junior trying out for quarterback, and you've got a heckuva stronger arm. The other two are just freshmen. Coach *never* plays freshmen."

"Well, we'll find out tomorrow." Matt smiled and swatted Martin on the shoulder. "Tell you what, I'm buying at the Dairy Barn after we shower, okay? Anything you want, so long as it doesn't cost more than 75 cents."

"You're on."

■

Martin picked up Matt at 7:55 the next morning, and they drove to the field house in silence. Matt ran his fingers through his wiry black hair, rubbed his face and absently chewed his lip.

For nearly two dozen players around the message board, it was the end of the world. As Martin and Matt drove up, they could see the expressions on other ex-teammates as they walked dejectedly back to their cars. No one enjoyed the idea of playing junior varsity.

"Whups, there's Vince. And David. And A.J. and Boz," Matt muttered. "That's practically the whole team I played with yesterday. Great, just great."

The two guys threaded their way through the throng around the message board. Each varsity position was listed two-deep, though a few had three names. Matt and Martin squinted to see the list.

Blind choice:
Without looking ahead, turn to page 15 or page 23 to see if Matt's name is on the list.

"No can do, Dee Dee," Matt said.

"Dad's got some work that's gotta be done, and he's countin' on me. I can't let him down. You know," Matt dropped his voice, "things haven't been all that easy on the old man since Mamma left. I gotta be there."

"Me too, Dee Dee," Martin chimed in. "We'll be leaving as soon as he gets off work and won't get back 'til Sunday. But hey! Thanks for inviting us."

"Well, okay," Dee Dee said suspiciously. "It's your loss, I guess." He got in his car and thundered off without another word.

Martin and Matt looked at each other.

"So, where d'ya wanna go all day Saturday, Marty?" Matt asked.

"Don't matter to me—so long as it's a long way from town."

■

Late Sunday afternoon, Matt and Martin were walking toward First Church for the evening service when a carload of football players screeched to a halt by them.

"Yo, Matt! Martin! You dumb bunnies missed the party of the year, man!"

"I'm tellin' ya, guys, there was more booze and broads than I've ever seen in one place in my life. It was awesome!"

"Yeah, and guess what, Matt-baby? Ol' Genie Salat was askin' 'bout you. She's got the hots for you big-time. Why don'cha give her a call?"

"Man, you shoulda seen me and Soozi! That woman was hot putty in my hands."

Matt smiled uneasily. He didn't like the way this conversation was going.

What would you do?
If Matt plays along with the stories, turn to page 25.
If Matt tries to avoid the subject, turn to page 48.

In the rage of the moment Matt whipped off his helmet and began beating the player. It took two referees to pull him off and the Eagles were assessed two 15-yard penalties for unsportsman-like conduct and fighting. Matt was ejected from the game.

The opposing team scored, but the Eagles held on to win 21 to 14.

After the game, Coach Dallas took Matt aside.

"Just what are you trying to prove, son?" Dallas shouted. "Forget the fact that we nearly lost the most important game of the season. What kind of witness is this for the leader of the church youth group and the founder of the Christian athletes' fellowship?"

"Look Coach, it wasn't my fault. What do you want from me? I'm not perfect. There was just one perfect man and they crucified him!"

"I'm not asking you to be perfect Matt. Just responsible. A lot of people look up to you. In your position in a town this size, you're a role model, whether you like it or not."

"Aw, Coach, don't give me that. I'm not a role model. I'm just a team player. Nobody looks up to me. That's crazy." Matt walked away.

Matt decided to walk home after he'd showered and dressed. On one street a few blocks from his house, several smaller kids were playing football under the street lights. As he passed, the game deteriorated into a shouting-and-pushing match. Two boys got into a swinging fight.

Matt jumped between them and pulled the two apart. "Hey, what's going on here? Why are you two fighting?"

The smaller boy pointed at the larger boy.

"Oh, he thinks he's Matt Brand when he plays quarterback. And all he wants to do is fight!"

Matt froze in his tracks. The blood rushed to his head. Coach Dallas' words came back to him in a heartbeat. Stunned, he let the two boys go.

"Danny, you can't be the quarterback anymore if you're gonna keep on hittin' people—or I'll take my football and go home. You hear me, Danny? I'm serious."

Matt walked away. But the boy's words stayed with him a long, long time.

The End

After the last bell rang, Matt went out to the field where the cross country team met. He watched as several guys stretched out around a light pole near the track.

Naw, he thought. It's just not what I want to do. Besides, it won't do much for my upper-body strength. And I *need* that if I'm going to make the football team next year.

Matt shook his head as he walked away. Nope, I'm just gonna have to work out on my own.

■

Johnny Watson was a jolly, round little man. He had an old service station he'd converted into a boxing ring and gym. He didn't make much money at it. But then, Johnny didn't need much money.

"No, that's too much weight too soon," he said as Matt strained to lift the weights. "Better to lift less weight, more times. Power lifting ... that comes later. If you stick with it, that is. Most don't."

One day several weeks later, Martin stopped by to see his sweating friend.

"Looking good, Matt. Those gym shorts really become you. I always said you look good in apricot," he said with mock flattery.

Watson walked in, his eyes fixed on Matt. "Good, good. You sticking to that diet I gave you? Lots of fiber, lots of protein. We'll bulk you up in no time, believe me."

He turned to Martin. "How about you, Garcia? Ready to get in shape?"

"Oh, no thank you, Mr. Watson. I have enough trouble fighting off the girls as it is now. You start putting muscles on my naturally sleek and sinewy body ... well, I shudder to think of the consequences!"

Matt and Martin walked outside so Matt could cool off.

"Gotta hand it to you, Matt. You've really been sticking with this fitness routine. I can already tell you've added muscle in your arms. Is it hard to stick with it?"

Matt stretched a calf muscle. "It wasn't—not at first anyway. But the past week or so, I'm finding myself, I dunno, losing interest—especially the daily stuff. If you'd arrived 30 minutes earlier, I think I could've been talked into heading to the Dairy Barn for a chocolate peanut butter malt."

THE OPTION PLAY 11

"Hey, twist my arm. What about the youth group trip to Beaumont tomorrow? You going?"

"Aw, I don't know, Marty. I want to be with Gaile and you guys. But I shouldn't miss working out. I feel obligated to, but it's just so ... so ... "

"Meaningless? boring? repetitious? macho? sweaty? stinky?" Martin offered.

"Yeah. All of them sometimes, and none of them sometimes. Know what I mean? Just why am I doing this?"

"Well, I thought you decided on a workout program to stay in shape for football next year—and to keep your weight up. I'd say you're doing a pretty good job on the weight stuff. You don't look half like the skeleton you used to."

"Flattered, I'm sure. But I'm serious Martin. If fun things like the Beaumont trip keep coming up, I'm going to have to make a decision. Should I go with the fun life or stick with this and turn into a sun-bronzed Greek god?"

"Can't you just be a Greek god on weekdays and a toad on weekends?"

What would you do?

If Matt sticks with the fitness program, turn to page 86.
If he decides to drop it, turn to page 91.

The following day after school, Matt asked Genie to return his JV jacket.

Having been dumped once already, Gaile wasn't ready to renew their relationship. And with Martin still feeling abandoned, Matt grew closer to the other football players, particularly those who partied a lot.

Matt still refused the beer and mixed drinks that came his way, but the pressure never let up. And no one was more vocal than James. Genie never gave James a second glance after dating Matt. She was tired of drunken wrestling matches in cars. She still liked Matt. And James knew it.

■

This time the party was at Dee Dee's house, though it spilled out into the yard as well. Bink came through with another cooler full of beer and began passing out can after can.

"C'mon Matt, one won't hurtcha," Bink slurred.

"Naw, thanks, Bink. I'm fine."

"And I say you're a gutless wonder, rookie," James boomed, silencing the party.

Matt smiled at James. Now what?

"You heard me," James roared—watching Genie out of the corner of his eye. "You're some kind of Jesus freak who don't touch beer, ain'cha? Then you laugh and tell all your religious friends what drunks and boozers we are, don'cha Brand?"

"Aw, James, you're drunk. You know I wouldn't say nothing like that. Besides, not everybody on the team drinks."

"Shuddup, punk. And I say you're lyin'. From now on, either you drink with the men or play patty-cake with the church boys and girls. But if you're too good to drink with us, then you're not welcome at our parties." James spit the words.

Matt looked around. The other players stared at him, not willing to commit. Genie started crying and stepped to the back of the room.

"Now, now, James, nobody's gettin' run out of the party," Bink said. "Here's the deal." He held up a six-pack he grabbed from the kitchen. "Matt chugs this six-pack, he's one of us. He don't, he ain't. Fair enough?"

"Yeah!" screamed the football players in unison. "Chug-a-lug!" they chanted. "Chug-a-lug!"

"Your choice, pretty boy," James said, his voice dripping with acid. "Drink the beer, or take a hike."

What would you do?
If Matt accepts the challenge, turn to page 68.
If he turns it down, turn to page 93.

Matt got that sinking feeling in his gut when he knew he'd been wrong.

"You're right Coach," he said, "I haven't given it my best today. I'm sorry. It won't happen again."

Coach O'Hara was taken aback by Matt's words. Then she noticed the other swimmers all listening.

"Hey, what is this? A free show? Do I look like a sideshow attraction? Swimmers swim! So, do it!"

■

Matt's times continued to improve over the season. He never won, but he came closer with each race.

At the district meet, Matt edged out a swimmer from Buna High School to finish sixth in the butterfly. That enabled Matt to earn a varsity letter for winning a point in the district meet.

As he hugged the side of the swimming pool, Coach O'Hara knelt down and whispered in his ear. "Matt, I've never been as proud of a swimmer as I am of you today. You always had the potential. Now I see you have the heart for it too. Congratulations. And If you come out for the swimming team again next year, I'll teach you some *real* swimming!"

Matt laughed and rubbed his sore muscles. I've got time for a couple of practice laps before the next heat starts, he thought.

Humming happily, Matt pushed off and methodically began swimming up and down the pool, lost in his private thoughts—and prayers—of thanksgiving.

The End

"Matt! You're it! You got it!" Martin whooped and pounded his friend on the back.

Sure enough, there was his name, "Matt Brand," listed second under "Quarterback." Matt stood there a moment. Suddenly, James Lively pushed through the crowd. He stood menacingly in front of Matt. The crowd quieted. Everyone had seen Lively cursing as he'd run up and down the bleachers yesterday.

James scowled at Matt for a heartbeat, then his face split into a smile. "Welcome to the NFL, boy," he said and stuck out his giant paw.

Matt's heart resumed its tempo. "Thanks," he mumbled before the other boys came up and congratulated him.

While he was busy talking, he didn't notice Martin scan the list. There it was, under "Center," the third name listed: "Martin Garcia." He clenched his fist in celebration, then joined the other guys around Matt. It was good they'd still be together.

By 8:05, only the varsity players remained.

James and first-team quarterback Dee Dee Morris sauntered up.

"Hey, rooks, we're having a party at Dee Dee's tonight. Whole team's invited," James said. "Be there. We're going to party our way to district! What d'ya say?"

The other guys cheered. Martin glanced at Matt. Dee Dee and James' parties were legendary. Neither Matt nor Martin had ever had a prayer of being invited to one before. All the best-looking, most popular girls would be there. And James' dad always provided the booze. *Lots* of booze.

Dee Dee stilled the celebration with his hands.

"As of this moment, we're all in this together. We're a team, see? We stick together. The only way this team is going to win district is if we work together. Last year's team didn't do that. I know. That's why we fell apart against Kirbyville and Newton. Well, I'm a senior. So are James and Bink and Dick. This is our last chance to go to district, to get noticed by the college scouts."

"Yeah, and we ain't lettin' nothing get in our way this time," James said, glaring around the crowd.

When he got to Matt, his gaze seemed to linger an extra fraction of a second. "Not nothing, not nobody is standing in our way. We're the Eagles! Right? I said, 'Right!?' " he roared. The other 47 players howled in unison.

Matt caught Martin's eye again and they slipped to the edge of the group.

"What're we going to do about the party?" Matt asked in a near whisper. "I hear there's lots of drinking and smoking pot, and the girls get pretty wild at some of those parties. What d'ya think?"

Martin shrugged helplessly. "I dunno. I'm not sure it's right for me to go. I don't know how it'd affect my witness."

"But do we really have a choice?" Matt asked. "I mean if we don't go, the whole team's gonna turn against us before we ever play a down of varsity football. We'll *never* be Eagles!"

What would you do?

If Matt goes to the party, turn to page 99.
If Matt doesn't go to the party, turn to page 103.

The next morning, Matt sought out Johnny Watson. "Did you hear what happened to Overstreet?" he asked.

"Yeah, wotta waste. Kid took too much stuff, too long. Prob'ly did it on his own too. Didn't have an expert like me tellin' him how much to take—or when. Let me tell you something, Brand. I care 'bout all youse kids. I wouldn't let nothin' happen to any of ya. Nobody's gonna die while Uncle Johnny's around, hear?"

"Yeah, I hear, Johnny," Matt mumbled. He liked what was happening to him on and off the field too much to give it up.

Outside the gym, Genie honked the horn. "Come on, Matt! We'll be late for school!"

Matt's junior year was a smashing success. When Dee Dee went down with a hip injury, Matt stepped in and led the Eagles to five consecutive victories and a play-off berth. He kept using steroids through the summer under Johnny's watchful eye.

His senior year was even better. Dave Campbell's Texas High School Football magazine called him the state's leading "blue-chip" recruit. Matt started on both offense and defense, and college coaches streamed to his school each week. Matt enjoyed every minute of it.

Recruiting continued into the spring, and Matt finally chose the best-known football power in the state of Oklahoma.

The night before national signing day for high school recruits, the head coach of the University of Southern Oklahoma sat in Matt's den with him and his father.

"Okay Matt, that about takes care of everything," the coach said. "The press will be here about 9 a.m. to record you signing on the dotted line here. Then I've gotta catch a plane to Waco for another blue-chipper. You'll like this kid, Matt. He's a 6-foot 5-inch, 280-pound lineman. Can't have too many of those, can you?"

They all laughed.

The coach routinely asked the last couple of questions on the letter of intent.

"Ever been arrested?"

"No."

"Did Southern Oklahoma offer you any money or inducements to sign?"

"No."

"Are you now, or have you ever taken anabolic steroids?"

Long pause.

The coach looked up. "Matt? Did you hear that one?"

What would you do?

If Matt tells the coach the truth, turn to page 28.

If he tells a lie, turn to page 45.

Matt gritted his teeth, unclenched his fists and walked up to the tight end. "God loves you." Matt then turned and walked off.

The tight end was speechless.

Following the game, Matt was walking to his car when Dee Dee came running up.

"Hey, Matt, wait up!" Matt turned to face Dee Dee. "I heard about what you said to that guy after that cheap shot he gave you. Man, I don't know how you did it."

"I didn't do it, Dee Dee," Matt said. "I'm not strong enough. I had to have help."

"Help?" Dee Dee was confused.

"Yep. You'll probably think I'm some kind of religious fanatic for saying this, but I prayed—before the game and all during the game—that God would help me control my temper. And he did!"

Dee Dee scratched his neck. "You really believe this Christian stuff, don't you?"

"Yeah, I do. Trouble is, just believing isn't enough. I still fail miserably—like I did against Buna. Like I do every day, actually. But God forgives me, and I start over again."

Dee Dee looked away from Matt's eyes. "I know some of the things I do aren't right. I know I shouldn't get drunk, fool around or take drugs. I feel so bad afterward. You know? It's fun while I'm doin' that stuff, but then I feel bad for days. I've done some bad stuff, Matt."

"So have we all, Dee Dee, so have we all. Even my pastor. We all mess up. We're human. But Jesus forgives us if we ask him to and stop doing stuff that's wrong. Really, he does—every time."

Dee Dee looked straight into Matt's eyes for a moment. "I'd like to know this Jesus the way you do," he said in a vulnerable, almost childlike voice.

Matt held back a laugh. "Great! All you gotta do is ask. C'mon. I'll introduce you to him over a chocolate peanut butter malt down at the Dairy Barn. My treat."

The End

Matt let out a sigh. "Maybe you're right," he admitted. "No coach would let his feelings hurt his team—not even Coach Charles. If he gave the job to Ky, then he must really believe Ky is the better quarterback. I think he's wrong, but my opinion doesn't count."

"So what're you going to do now?"

"Good question. Football's all I've ever done except play baseball in the spring. I do know I'm *not* playing on JV again this year. That's just too humiliating for a junior."

"Well, what else do you do in the off-season to stay in shape?" Robyn prodded.

"Mostly just run or work out in the weight room. Sometimes both. Sometimes neither."

"Well, you could try other sports. For example, you say you run to stay in shape. Then why not try out for cross country? Or if you'd rather lift weights, develop your own workout program. Then you could try out for varsity again next year."

"Yeah, those both make sense. But which one should I do?" Matt asked.

"That's up to you, Matt."

What would *you* do?

If Matt tries out for the cross country team, turn to page 110.
If Matt develops his own fitness program, turn to page 10.

"Uh, hi Vernon!" Matt said, "We were just talking ... "

"About dumb jocks, I know. I heard," Vernon said. "Matt, you're setting yourself up for some grief if you keep talking like that. Some of that stuff's already gotten back to the football team. Guys like Bink and James don't take too kindly to it."

When he saw he wasn't in danger of having his face rearranged, Matt grew bold once again. "So what? They know it's true."

"Matt, what you say about them affects all of us," Vernon said. "You don't know anything about me, do you?"

Matt thought a moment. "No, not really."

"I took both the ACT and the SAT this fall. I scored high enough to get into Rice, Baylor, Vanderbilt or Duke. I'm gonna graduate with high honors. And guess what? I play football."

"I ... never knew," Matt said.

"You're only hurting yourself when you talk about people you don't know. I know you're the leader of the youth group at First Church. Well, I'm a Christian too, Matt. I go to Holiness Fellowship. On the football team there are Christians and non-Christians and everything in between. There are scholars and guys who can't read or write. There are blacks and whites and a couple of guys who're a little of both. And you're blowing my chances to reach any of these guys."

Matt felt his stomach sink. "Oh, uh, like, I ... didn't realize." Matt took a deep breath. "Vernon, I'm sorry. I was stupid. I guess I need to get to know you guys better and quit mouthin' off."

"So why not try out for the team again?" Vernon asked. "No better way to get to know the players."

"Yeah, that may be true, but I could probably get to know more athletes without playing on the team, couldn't I? By going to more events or something?"

"Maybe, I dunno. That's up to you. But if you worked hard enough, I bet you could make the team again."

What would you do?

If Matt gets to know more athletes, turn to page 70.
If he gets involved in sports again, turn to page 85.

Who needs this grief? Matt thought.

He looked back up at Coach O'Hara. "Maybe you're right Coach," he said politely. "Can't get blood from a turnip. And after eight consecutive last-place finishes, I'm not sure I'll ever be a swimmer. But thanks for trying anyway."

Matt got out of the pool and never came back.

After a few weeks off, Matt began to get in shape again for one last stab at football. He ran each day in the pine forest that surrounded the town, watched his diet and practiced throwing passes with his father. Next year Matt would be a senior. It'd be his last chance.

Two-a-day practices began again in August, and among those trying for a spot on the varsity was Ky Sams. Matt and Ky were locked in a struggle to see who'd come out first-string quarterback.

As usual, Coach Charles kept mum about the whole thing. On the morning after the last two-a-days, he posted the varsity roster on the bulletin board outside the field house. Matt's heart pounded as he wondered whether he'd once again face disappointment.

Blind choice:

Without looking ahead, turn to page 104 or page 24 to see if Matt makes the team.

Matt looked under "Quarterback." Dee Dee Morris was listed first, followed by Ky Sams. Matt stood frozen in his spot, staring at the board. Martin peered around him. His name wasn't listed under "Center" either.

Around them, the guys who'd made varsity for the first time were celebrating, pounding each other on the back.

Dee Dee and James pressed through the crowd.

"Listen up boys!" James roared. "Me 'n' Dee Dee are havin' a get-acquainted party at Dee Dee's house tonight. And *all* the fightin' Eagles *will* be there!"

The team howled in unison. Dee Dee's parties were notorious. All the best-looking girls, all the best liquor, all the best *everything* would be there.

"Tonight, we're a team," Dee Dee said over the tumult. "We think like a team, we act like a team, we play like a team." He paused for effect. "And tonight we party like a team!"

The Eagles, old and new, thundered their approval.

Matt and Martin tried to slip away. But before they could leave the crowd, James pushed his way in front of them.

He stared at Matt. "This party is for men only," he sneered. "You JV boys can come back and try again next year."

Matt barely heard him. He was lost in his own thoughts. He started to push past James' broad shoulders, but James grabbed a handful of shirt and held him close. The guys all grew quiet as they watched.

"You tried to make me look bad yesterday with that sneaky stuff, boy," he hissed through clenched teeth. "We got business to settle."

Matt shook himself free and stared up at James.

"No thanks. I got something better to do," he said, his voice barely audible, before walking off.

James stood dumbfounded. Nobody ever walked off from James Lively.

"C'mon Martin," Matt said. "I need to think about the coaches' decision."

What would you do?

If Matt decides to accept the coaches' decision, turn to page 46.
If Matt blows a fuse at their decision, turn to page 75.

With a whoop and a holler that could be heard clear to the courthouse square, Matt jumped straight up in the air, pumping his fist. He was the starting quarterback! He'd made it!

Matt worked even harder in the days before the first game against the Buna High School Bumblebees. His first start was a solid—if not spectacular—performance. Matt completed 10 of 18 passes for 88 yards and rushed for 69 more as the Eagles defeated the Bees 22 to 16.

In the euphoria of the locker room after the game, Matt found a quiet corner of the shower and let the hot water beat on his face. He reflected on the events of the past year—good and bad—and saw that God had led him to this moment.

After the shower, Matt went in the laundry room for a moment and prayed silently: Thanks for the chance to play, for even being able to play. Thanks for sticking with me when I let you down. Thanks for giving me a will to succeed. And thanks for letting me accomplish my goals. Oh yeah, please forgive me when I put those goals ahead of what you know is best for me. Amen.

When he looked up, Matt saw that Martin had been standing behind him. He blushed, but Martin smiled.

"How about a peanut butter chocolate malt at the Dairy Barn to celebrate, Mr. Brand?" Martin asked. "My treat."

"That, Mr. Garcia, is an offer that's too good to pass up."

Matt was so happy that he drank two malts and had an order of fries on the side. He and Martin talked for hours after that game. They talked about football and about the coach. But mostly they talked about how God had kept Matt going.

And they dreamed about just where God would take them next. After high school, after college—and beyond. But, in the end, they didn't come to any great conclusions about the future. Except that God would be there with them.

And that was enough.

The End

"Like I said, Mattie-boy, the thing you missed was little Miss Genie," Bink said with a leer. "Friday night coulda been *your* night, Brand."

"Aw, g'wan, guys. Genie likes them big, muscular dudes. Like James Lively," Matt said.

"That could be you," Bink said mysteriously. "Listen, we're heading down to Johnny Watson's gym. Why not come along? We'll fill you in on the party. That is, unless, you've got someplace more important to go."

Martin started to walk away. "Actually, Bink, we were going to ..." but Matt cut him off. "Yeah, sure, count us in."

Martin glared at Matt.

"Look, we're already suspect 'cause we missed the party," Matt whispered. "Let's not make it worse by telling the guys we're going to church. They're tryin' to include us."

"Okay, boys," Bink said, "hop in."

At Watson's Gym, Bink took Matt aside. "Matt, I wanna show you something. You wanna know why SMU and A&M have scouts at our games? Look at this." Bink pulled his T-shirt off and flexed his muscles. They rippled likes swells in the ocean. Matt was amazed. He'd never noticed Bink's physique before. The guy was huge.

"Girls like 'em, coaches like 'em, scouts like 'em," Bink said with a wink. "You're going to be starting quarterback next year. We've got to start getting you beefed up now. With a little help, you'll be able to throw further than Dee Dee ever could. And that stuff we said about Genie was true. I think she could go for you in a big way—if you play your cards right."

Matt started to protest but was interrupted by several other guys who came bounding up. "C'mon, Matt ol' son, let's hit the weights." Two of the players pulled off their shirts to reveal similar muscle tone. Without warning, Bink pulled Matt's shirt up and slapped his ribs.

"Rookie, you're gonna hafta put some meat on your bones if you're gonna play in the big leagues," he said. "And I ain't talkin' about football neither."

The other players laughed. Matt could feel his neck and cheeks turning red.

"All right. I give up. I'm convinced. I'll hit the weights. But I warn you. It'll take a powerful lot of weightlifting to change a

natural pencil-shape like me."

Bink looked at the other players, then exploded into laughter. "You really don't know, do you rook? No, I guess you don't. Brand, let me explain something. You don't get muscles like this just by pumping iron. You could do bench presses and free weights forever, and you'd still be a toothpick. You need some of this."

He held out a small bottle of pills. " 'Roids, man. Use them and they'll bulk you up in no time."

"Steroids?" Matt said stupidly. "What . . . what does Coach think about this? I mean, I've heard that they mess with your skin, make you break out. And some people say they make you meaner, almost crazy. Haven't you heard any of that stuff?"

"Boy, you're dumb, Brand," Bink said with a snort of disgust. "College coaches *want* mean, aggressive players. Everybody uses steroids. Besides, all that stuff quits when you stop taking them.

"Anyway, who do you think suggested we come to Johnny Watson in the first place? An alumni of one of the state schools who's real tight with the recruiters. So c'mon, Brand, what d'ya say?"

What would you do?

If Matt accepts the steroids, turn to page 82.
If Matt turns down the steroids, turn to page 88.

"Matt?"

"I've gotta confess something here—to both of you." Matt turned to his father. "Dad, I've been on steroids for more than a year. I wanted to stop, but I was afraid to. Afraid I'd lose my chance to play college ball. I wanted you to be proud of me." He couldn't hold back the tears. He knew this would mean no scholarship. And he knew he was hurting his dad.

"I was afraid of that," the coach said. "Your growth has been too fast, too pronounced. Trouble is, if I don't sign you someone else will, and I'd never live that down."

Matt looked up. "What do you want me to do?"

"Just sign the paper, Matt," the coach said wearily, "and stop using that darn stuff as of right now. Drug testing at Southern Oklahoma is sporadic at best. This'll give you a few months to get the steroids out of your system. And once you get to school I'll try to warn you whenever there's rumors of random testing. That okay with you?"

"Yeah, that's great," Matt said, smiling. But his father continued to scowl.

■

Matt had a spectacular August at Southern Oklahoma and made the team as a backup quarterback as a freshman. He played the fourth quarter of an opening game rout of Texas A&M and threw a touchdown in his first collegiate game. The campus—and the press—went crazy over the humble, muscular kid from East Texas with a left arm like a bazooka.

Wednesday afternoon after the game, there was a knock on Matt's dorm room door. It was a random drug test. Matt's phone began ringing. He knew it was the coach. He also knew the call was a couple of minutes too late.

Matt tested positive for steroids, along with two other players.

The University of Southern Oklahoma was banned from any bowl games or TV appearances for the next year. And the team was restricted in the number of high school players it could recruit for the next two years. The coach was fired shortly thereafter.

Matt never played another down of college ball. He dropped out of school midway through his sophomore season and went back to East Texas.

By the time the next season rolled around, no one even

remembered Matt Brand.

Except his dad. And his youth minister, Robyn. And God.

And together, they began to pick up the pieces of Matt's broken life. And start over.

The End

As soon as Coach Charles lit into Matt and the other team members, the rest of the party scattered.

"I ought to kick you all off the team. I really should," Charles said, barely controlling his anger. "But I don't have that luxury. Dee Dee, Matt, you boys know Ky's not ready to step in at quarterback. I can't believe you'd put me in a situation like this. I really can't.

"Get on the phone and call your parents right now. This party's over, and I don't want none of you drunkards driving yourselves home."

"Yes sir, Coach," the guys responded. Matt felt like he was going to throw up.

Then Coach Charles turned to Matt. "Oh, and one last thing, preacher boy. If I do decide to take you off the team, I don't want you tellin' your daddy or your little friends at First Church that I'm some big bad monster who ain't gonna let you play 'cause I don't like you. I want you to tell them why you're not playing. Got that? I said, 'Got that!?' "

"Yes sir, Coach!"

"Darn straight." Coach Charles spit out the door and then stormed out.

Matt slumped on the floor when Coach Charles left. After a moment, Martin slipped in and sat down beside him.

"Some witness this is," Matt said. "I can just see the sports headlines: 'First Church Youth Leader Sidelined for Drinking Violation.' Dad'll blister my hide—and I'll deserve it. Come on, let me have it. Say 'I told you so, Matt.' "

"Okay. I told you so, Matt. Now, what're we going to do about this?"

"What's there to do? It's done. I blew it."

"Matt, what happened tonight doesn't just affect you, you know. I'm a Christian too. And I'm your best friend. What you get labeled with, I get labeled with. And I don't want to be labeled a hypocrite. So I think we need to take a stand in front of the guys. Let them know how we really feel about this stuff."

"After what just happened? Martin, are you crazy? I've got zero credibility and respect on this team now. Zero! Nada! None!"

"Well, I can't say much for your timing," Martin said, "but it doesn't change things. Keeping quiet won't set this right."

"How? Hold Bible studies and prayer times before games?

Martin, I see your point, but maybe it'd be best just to, you know, lead by example. Saying anything right now will make me look like a total jerk."

"Not saying anything may have the same result. Matt, it's on your shoulders. You have to decide what's best to do."

What would you do?

If Matt and Martin make their beliefs known to the rest of the team, turn to page 66.

If Matt decides to just lead by example, turn to page 78.

Matt heaved himself out of the chair and stormed out the door. "Aw, you just don't understand Robyn. It isn't that simple!"

After a second, he got control of himself and peered back around the doorway into her office. "Uh, but thanks for tryin', anyway."

"Sure, Matt. Any time," Robyn said—mostly to herself.

Over the next couple of weeks, Matt stayed home after school, studying or watching old movies on television. He only ventured out on weekends to pick up his girlfriend Gaile Scarborough. They went to eat or watch movies in Beaumont so Matt could avoid seeing the guys on the team. Gaile kept her opinions of Matt's behavior to herself.

Sunday evening, Vinnie "The Studebaker" Cleagle, starting off guard with the Houston Rockets, spoke at First Church. The Studebaker grew up north of town, playing on the dozens of outdoor basketball courts that dotted the woods. He'd then gone on to play professional ball. During the NBA off-season, he'd become an in-demand speaker for his Christian testimony. Gaile managed to drag Matt to church to hear him. They sat in the back.

"Man, I was on top of the world when the Warriors drafted me," Cleagle said, prowling the platform like a caged panther. "Oh, I was hot stuff. Last pick of the first round. Big money. San Francisco. And me, little Vinnie Cleagle from East Texas. I thought I was going to take over the whole NBA.

"But it didn't work out that way. I sat. And sat. And sat. I played in only 37 games that year, mostly trash minutes when the game was already decided. In my best game I scored seven points against the Lakers. And that came when we were down by 42!

"Then, just before the next season started, the Warriors cut me loose. Made me a free agent. Me, The Studebaker! I thought my world had ended. I didn't wanna talk to nobody. I sulked. I pouted. I blamed God. I blamed the Warriors. I blamed everybody but Vinnie Cleagle.

"And when I was at my lowest, I sat on an empty basketball court near my parents' house and cried out, 'Why me, God? Why did you do this to me? Why did you leave me like this?'

"And in a way I can't explain to you, Jesus came to me. He bandaged my wounds. And spoke to me in love. He told me about my sin—the pride, the self-centeredness. And showed me a way out.

"The next day I started working out. I was determined to play pro basketball again. Not for fame. Not for money. But for God. A few months later, the Rockets signed me on as guard. I was a starter by year's end. In the last two years I've been second on the Rockets in scoring and played in an all-star game. And I praise God every opportunity I get."

The church erupted in applause. Matt sunk down in his chair. I understand what Vinnie's saying, he thought, but how does it affect me? It's too late to go out for the JV team. And just because it worked that way for Vinnie doesn't guarantee it'll work for me. Still, why is my heart beating so hard? Could God be trying to tell me something?

What would you do?

If Matt follows the speaker's example, turn to page 58.
If Matt decides the testimony doesn't apply to him, turn to page 114.

Matt stood behind his offensive line and surveyed the field, wiping his hands on the towel attached to his belt. This was his moment, the one he'd dreamed of since he played Peewee Football years ago. He waited until the last second before calling for the ball. Matt dumped a short pass off to the halfback circling out of the backfield for a 6-yard gain.

The game was a slugfest in the trenches. Matt kept the Panthers off balance with a series of draws, misdirection plays, short passes and screens. With the score tied in the last minute, Matt executed a bootleg around left end. It came down to a matchup between Matt and the same safety who'd taken Dee Dee out of the game earlier. This time, the hours of practice at weakside linebacker paid off. Matt lowered his shoulder and drove the safety into the end zone. The Eagles mobbed Matt, creating a 5-yard penalty for delay of game. But no one minded. And as the last seconds ticked off the clock, the other players carried him off the field.

Matt's conservative play-calling was just what the Eagles needed, and they began a winning streak that swept them through district, including a 28 to 6 romp over arch-rival Kirbyville.

Matt's stock soared on campus. The pastor of First Church mentioned him in a sermon. Even Ol' Lady O'Hara sometimes had something nice to say to him before English class.

Two more foes fell in the bi-district and regional games. Matt's precision passes and quick play-calling led the Eagles over several bigger, faster teams. Matt felt like he was living in a dream world. Even the games themselves seemed in slow motion.

The Eagles drew the powerful La Vega Pirates in a semifinal game. Matt's confidence was at an all-time high. Just moments before the game, Coach Charles called him over.

"Son, these guys are faster than anybody we've faced before. The past couple of weeks you've had a tendency to aim the ball. Can't do it against La Vega. Better our receivers drop a ball that's thrown too hard than take a chance on an interception. You hear me, Matt?"

"You bet, Coach," Matt said, the blood pumping so fiercely in his head that his skin felt like it was on fire.

La Vega was everything Coach Charles had said it would be—and more. Error-free football kept the Eagles in the game. Matt played well, zipping his passes just as Coach instructed. But in the end, La Vega won 10 to 6. Matt slumped on the bench and listened to the Pirates' celebration at midfield.

Martin walked up and sat by Matt as the rest of the team filed into the locker room. Martin could see his friend's hunched form as Matt buried his face in his own hands. For several minutes they sat there as the stands emptied.

"Matt, Matt, it's over. Over," Martin said. "But it was just a game, right? Not the end of the world."

What would you do?

If Matt deals with the defeat positively, turn to page 115.
If he deals with the defeat negatively, turn to page 108.

Matt continued to pray for guidance late into the evening. When he woke up the next morning, he knew what he had to do. He had to stop using steroids. Bink found out about it after a few days. But following Glenn Overstreet's death, he really couldn't say much.

Several weeks later, the school district superintendent called a meeting of all students involved in sports. They crowded into the high school auditorium. The school board president angrily recounted the anonymous tips he'd received from coaches at other schools that some members of the Eagle football team were taking steroids.

"First, I want you to know that I won't tolerate any kind of drug use," the president thundered. "Any student caught using steroids will be suspended. Second, we'll begin an immediate policy of mandatory drug testing to put these rumors to rest. Third, I want a unanimous show of support from the athletes whose reputations have been maligned. I'm passing around a sheet that states you are drug-free and you support mandatory drug testing. I want each of you to read it and sign it."

Several of the seniors jumped up and objected. As he watched, Matt wondered how long steroids would remain in his body after he'd quit using them.

Suddenly, Matt heard something strange amid the hubbub and looked at Martin, who was sitting to his left. Martin was sniffling, tears streaking down his cheeks.

"Martin, not you!" Matt gasped. "When did you start?"

"Last week," Martin said quietly. "Bink and some guys cornered me in the locker room. Said I was hurting the team if I didn't. Matt, will they kick me out of school if they find out? What am I going to do?"

Just then, the list was handed down the row to Matt. Coach Charles was standing at the end of the row, a black scowl on his face. The players sitting in front of Matt turned and stared at him as he held the long document.

Dear God, he prayed silently, desperately. What should I do?

What would you do?

If Matt supports the drug testing, turn to page 50.
If he opposes the drug plan, turn to page 55.

Using a series of misdirection plays, short passes and draws, Matt slowly moved the Eagles up the field against the Panthers. With each play, Matt's confidence increased.

Finally, at the 11-yard-line, Coach Charles sent in the next play with the split end. Charles wanted a safe option play off right tackle. But at the line of scrimmage, Matt saw that his wide receiver would have only man-to-man coverage. Matt paused a moment, then changed the play.

"Hut! Hut!" Matt danced back and waited for Tommy to break clear of the cornerback. C'mon Tommy, Matt thought. C'mon! C'mon!

Suddenly, a white light, then blackness.

Matt felt himself falling and the football tumbling in slow motion out of his grasp. A black-and-gold Panther jersey smothered it, and Matt hit the grass hard. The safety who'd sacked him from behind did a war dance over Matt's body.

As Matt stumbled toward the sidelines, he could see Coach Charles was livid. He grabbed Matt by the facemask and shook him angrily. "You changed my call, boy! What on earth were you thinking?"

"I saw ... single coverage on Tommy. He'd been beating that cornerback all day. I thought ... "

"You thought? No you didn't! Son, did it ever occur to you why there was single coverage? Because the safety was blitzing! Brand, that's why you'll never be anything more than a backup quarterback: You don't think!" Charles slapped Matt's helmet and stormed off.

Matt looked around. The whole team had heard the coach's outburst and looked away. The Eagles played listless football the rest of the evening and were beaten in the second half.

The next couple of weeks weren't any better. While Dee Dee recovered from a hip pointer, Matt tried to rally the team. But while the defense continued to play well, the offense didn't respond to Matt's leadership. The Eagles lost all three games. When Dee Dee finally returned, Coach Charles benched Matt, and he saw no more playing time that season.

The week of the final game, Matt stopped by his dad's office at the newspaper. "Dad, got a minute?"

"Sure, son. But why aren't you at football practice?"

"Aw, Dad, you know why. Coach Charles will never play me.

He hardly speaks to me since I got sacked against Center. I'm just wasting my time. I might as well save everybody some hassle and bug out."

"Hmm, I dunno, son," Matt's dad said. "Quitting now may not be the best thing. You quit once, and it gets easier and easier to quit again. Besides, there's only a week left. You quit now, and you've got no shot for next year. Period."

"But Dad, you don't know how humiliating it is to stand out there day after day and have the head coach ignore you. I can't take it anymore."

"Have you prayed about it?"

Matt paused. "No, not much, I guess."

"Tell you what. Pray about it. But you keep going out to practice until you hear from God what he wants you to do. And if you think you're not supposed to go out next year, I'll back you 100 percent. But if you think you're supposed to try out, I'll work with you myself in the off-season. Deal?"

"Deal."

■

By the end of the final game on Friday, Matt knew he needed to give his best to lay the groundwork for his senior year.

Matt's dad kept his word and took an hour out of his schedule almost every day to work out with his son. Their workouts soon took precedence over everything else. By summer, Matt was in the best condition of his life. He had the Eagle playbook memorized and, for the first time, felt confident in his abilities.

Matt arrived several minutes early for the first two-a-day workout. Only Coach Charles was there, scribbling something on his ever-present clipboard, already working on his first chaw of tobacco.

Matt walked up the stands to where Charles was sitting. Charles barely looked up from his clipboard.

"So you still want to be quarterback, huh, Brand? What makes you think I've forgotten how you tried to show me up last year against Center?"

That again? Surely Coach Charles had had plenty of time to cool off about that. Still, Matt was determined to give it his best shot.

Matt grinned. "I just want to play, Coach."

Matt walked on into the field house. *If I make it, I make it. And if I don't, well, at least I gave it my all. It's as simple as that.*

Blind choice:
Without looking ahead, turn to page 24 or page 43 to continue the story.

Genie stood so close Matt noticed there were flecks of gold in her hazel eyes.

"The guys tell me you're a pretty tough customer," she said.

"Well, I guess I hold my own," he said, being as casual as possible.

"Really, I remember that time in two-a-days when you got hit late and still completed a long pass."

"Yeah, well, I'm lucky. I'm blessed with a high pain threshold," Matt said. "I played practically the whole JV season last year with a bad knee. But you gotta do what you gotta do."

Wanda wasn't happy with the close quarters Genie was keeping. "What's this scar on your hand?" she asked, grabbing his hand in hers.

"Oh, that. Nothing really. I got spiked last year covering home during baseball season. Didn't get it sewed up until the next morning." Matt was liking the attention—a lot.

"That's right, ladies," James said, his words slurring as he walked up. "Matt's an iron man. I've given him my best shot. Guys just stood there and laughed at me. Isn't that right, Brand?"

"Uh, yeah, James. Sure, whatever you say."

James' voice iced up. "Not only that, the rookie here has a hollow leg. He can drink us all under the table. Can't you, Brand?" He stepped forward. Genie grabbed at James' arm, but he slapped it away. "I said, 'Can't you, Brand?' "

"Well, I dunno about that, James," Matt said, fully aware James was baiting him. "Now, you and Dee Dee—you guys are the best. Everybody knows that. Me? I'm just an amateur when it comes to beer-drinkin'."

"And I say you're too modest, rook," James said, his lips twisting into a sneer. "Here's a six-pack, already iced down. A man half as tough as you say you are should be able to chug-a-lug this baby in no time flat. What d'ya say?"

James stepped squarely in front of Matt, dangling the six-pack of beer. Matt could see most of the people in the room watching the scenario unfold. He could see Martin still standing wide-eyed in the doorway. Martin shook his head and mouthed the word "No!" He knew Matt didn't drink.

The music continued playing, but Matt couldn't hear it. Genie, Wanda, Therese, Soozi and the others watched him. This was his big—maybe his only—chance to be a part of the crowd. Besides, it would shut James up—once and for all. If he backed down now, James would never let up on him.

At the same time, he'd never had a beer in his life, and he was the leader of the church youth group. Kids looked up to him, trusted him.

Matt's mouth went very, very dry.

What would you do?

If Matt accepts the challenge, turn to page 68.
If Matt turns it down, turn to page 93.

Matt found his name on the roster, but he was listed third behind Ky and the promising quarterback from last year's freshman team. He'd already decided to bow out if he didn't make first or second string so he turned and walked back to his car. Martin, who'd also tried out, made second-string center.

Martin came running up. "I'm sorry Matt. I really am."

"So am I, in a way," Matt said. "But I think I knew, deep down inside, that I wasn't as good as the other guys. They deserve the chance. And hey! I'm a senior. It's going to be a very busy year. You ready for it?"

"You bet!" Martin beamed, and they drove off together to the first day of classes.

Matt's senior year was indeed busy. With the help of Robyn McGregor, the youth minister, the youth group at First Church continued to grow. Over Christmas break, the group went on its first mission trip to Matamoros, Mexico. Later, it even sponsored its first concert, bringing Billy Crockett to sing at the church.

In school, Matt was named editor of the school newspaper, and he found he liked journalism better than just about any other class. Maybe he'd be a reporter some day. After all, that's what his dad did now. He concentrated more on his classes, knowing he'd need good grades to get into the college of his choice.

And then there were weekends when he'd just go walking or shopping with his girlfriend, Gaile, or Martin—or sometimes both. The times they spent talking about life were among the best times of all.

One day in November as the three of them were in a new mall in Beaumont, Martin asked, "Matt, do you miss football?"

Matt stopped and turned and looked at his friends. "A little. But somewhere down the line God taught me that football's not everything.

"I think athletics are great. But you just can't put them first in your life. I'm trying hard to put Jesus first and everything else second in my life. But boy! Do I screw up sometimes!"

Matt paused, embarrassed by the intensity of his emotions.

"Sorry. I'm sure you guys weren't expecting a sermon. I guess I do that a lot these days, huh?"

But Gaile and Martin smiled. Both hugged him.

"Aw, big guy, you'll always be a star to us," Gaile said. "Even if the only passing you do this year is calculus!"

They laughed and walked—with arms locked—out of the mall toward Matt's car in the parking lot.

The End

▼

"Uh, yeah, steroids, right?" Matt stumbled. "No, I never took 'em."

But the damage was already done. The coach, already suspicious, checked with Coach Charles the next morning. When he examined Matt's development chart, he saw the growth pattern that began during his junior year. He called Matt that afternoon.

"Sorry son. It looks too suspicious for me to take a chance on you," he said. "The NCAA is really cracking down on steroid use. If you turned up positive in some random drug test, we could be in big trouble. I'm going to have to withdraw our scholarship offer."

Somehow word of Matt's alleged steroid use got around and no other schools offered him a scholarship either. Matt eventually went to his father's college, but was forced to work part time to make ends meet.

He continued to play football for fun and eventually stopped taking steroids. The bulking effects of the steroids wore off as quickly as they'd come. Within a year, Matt was looking like his old self again. But the pain that resulted from his choices stayed with him a long, long time.

The End

At lunch time, Martin found Matt sitting in a corner of the cafeteria, an untouched sandwich and apple sitting on the table.

"Mind if I join you?"

Matt kept looking straight ahead.

"Don't mind if I do," Martin said as he sat down beside Matt. "Now, let's see what culinary delights are hidden within the confines of this humble brown sack. Ooo! *Croissant au fromage, une pomme et le lait!* Aren't we the lucky campers!?"

Matt continued his stony silence, staring blankly.

"Actually, I'd trade with you Matt, but we haven't gotten to 'tuna fish' yet in French class, so I don't know how to ask."

Still nothing.

Martin leaned over the table and peered right into Matt's face.

"Hello? Hey, I know you're bummed. But you go into Ol' Lady O'Hara's class playing 'I Was a Teenage Zombie,' and you'll get your fanny in very hot water. *Tu comprends?*"

Slowly, recognition dawned in Matt's eyes.

"I'm serious, Matt."

"Yeah, I know. I guess I've been thinking and praying about what happened today."

"And what did you come up with, Einstein?"

"Ky looked good out there. He moved the second-team offense better than I did. Nearly every time."

"So? You've got twice the arm he's got. He couldn't hit Ol' Lady O'Hara. From the first row. With a beach ball."

For the first time, Matt smiled.

"Wouldn't have mattered. He wouldn't have had time to throw against Lively and them on defense anyway. Ky's quicker. He knew he had to do a lot of roll-outs and misdirection plays. I tried to sit in the pocket and dazzle with my pinpoint passing like some junior league Dan Marino. They clobbered me. Ky took what was given him and made something out of it."

"Yeah, but if you'd had a chance to work behind the 'A-Team' line instead of skinny little bozos like me, you could've showed Coach something."

"No, the coaches made the right decision. This time, anyway. Now the next decision is up to me."

"What decision is that?" Martin asked between bites of cheese sandwich.

"Look at this skinny body of mine. I have a tendency to

wither away fast if I don't work out. Remember how I shriveled up last year when I hurt my ankle? I need some kind of activity or I'll end up a human toothpick. And I *refuse* to endure the humiliation of playing JV my junior year."

"You want to run faster, right? So try out for cross country. The team meets for the first time after school today."

"Cross country." Matt grinned. "That might be fun. Let's see, I've got three class periods to make up my mind."

What would you do?

If Matt goes out for the cross country team, turn to page 110.
If he decides to take another route, turn to page 10.

For a while, Matt tried to avoid the more explicit discussions. But he finally gave in and laughed and joked with the guys—anything to be included. Soon Bink and James were telling him about their latest sexual exploits—in graphic detail.

And everybody laughed as the church bells began to chime.

■

The gross conversations didn't end that Sunday, however. The locker rooms before and after the practices and games were the worst. The other players told both Matt and Martin far more than they ever wanted to know about certain girls, certain parties—even certain drugs. And the language often made them shudder, particularly when the Lord's name was abused.

Eventually both Matt and Martin sought Robyn McGregor's advice.

Robyn squeezed a second chair in front of her desk in the youth minister's tiny office. Soon both guys were emotionally describing how uncomfortable they felt being considered "one of the guys."

"Guys, this is a tough one," Robyn said. "No one wants to be laughed at or rejected. But some things are important to Christians. Just as Bink wouldn't want you talking about his mother or sister, you're not wild about him talking about your heavenly father that way, right?"

"But what can we do, Robyn?" Matt pleaded. "Some things they say make me sick to my stomach—and I don't consider myself a prude."

"Do the other guys know how you two feel, Martin?"

"No, I guess not. Some of them know we go to church, but that's about all," he said. "It just seems kinda late to stand up and say, 'Hey! You know all that stuff you guys have been tellin' us? Well, we only pretended we were interested. And as of this minute we don't want to hear it anymore. Okay?' "

"You may be right, Martin, but there are other things you can do," Robyn said. "Trouble is, they're not a whole lot easier."

"Yeah? Like what?" Matt asked.

"At some point you're going to have to make it known you're Christians. In other words, you're going to have to take a public stand for Jesus Christ. On the football field. In the locker room. In the classroom. And the sooner you do it, the better. The longer you're part of the sexual talk, the harder it'll be for anyone to take you seriously when you do take a stand."

Robyn's words stung Matt. He felt himself blushing. "What you're asking is too hard, Robyn. We're not martyrs—we're just kids. Teenagers!"

"What did you think, Matt?" Robyn asked. "That you could wait until you're an adult to act like a Christian? That you could sort of put your faith on hold until you graduate from college?"

"No! Yes! I mean, I dunno," Matt sputtered. "I don't know what to do. Maybe just leading by example would be enough, don't you think?"

"Maybe. Maybe not," Robyn said. "That's your decision."

What would you do?

If Matt and Martin make their faith known to the rest of the team, turn to page 66.

If they decide to try to lead quietly by example, turn to page 78.

If Matt and Martin make their faith known to the rest of the team, turn to page 66.

If they decide to try to lead quietly by example, turn to page 78.

Matt scanned the players around him. Fully half were using steroids. Some of these guys are going to be dead soon if they keep this up, he thought.

"What'll it be Brand?" Coach Charles asked.

Matt stared at Charles. "I'm signing, Coach."

■

Later that week the tests were administered. It took a week for the results to get back from Beaumont. On the day the tests were to be returned, Matt and Martin sat together at lunch.

"Look, you only took them a couple of days, and you stopped immediately," Matt argued, "and we tried to flush them out of your system right away. I've never seen a guy drink so much water! I thought you'd float off! Besides, these tests were designed to catch long-term users like Bink."

Martin only stared at his half-eaten sandwich.

The door to the cafeteria flew open. In the doorway stood Coach Charles with a letter in his hand.

"I need to see these students in the principal's office," he said. The list of names included both Bink and Martin. The students shuffled out. Their tests had proven positive.

After a minute, Dee Dee and Vernon walked up and sat by Matt as the rest of the students remained frozen in silence.

"That's half the team," Dee Dee told Matt, the fear obvious in his voice. "We'll get killed this week in Kirbyville."

Matt continued to stare at the now-empty doorway.

"Listen. My dad says we can file a lawsuit challenging the legality of the mandatory tests," Dee Dee said. "We can get an injunction prohibiting the school district from suspending any of the players until a judge has heard both sides of the argument. And that could take weeks. What d'ya think?"

"Those guys are guilty," Vernon said. "I told Bink to stay away from that stuff. He's just going to have to take his lumps."

Dee Dee and Vernon glared at each other, then Dee Dee asked, "Matt, you're for stalling this junk, aren't you?"

What would you do?

If Matt accepts the results of the tests, turn to page 56.
If Matt joins the lawsuit challenging the tests, turn to page 71.

Three weeks into the cross country season, Matt met with his youth minister one evening after a grueling practice.

"I'm sorry, Robyn," Matt said, still sweating from that evening's run. "I'm going to have to step down as youth group president. I never dreamed cross country would take this much time. We never get home until dark, and then I have to do my homework, or my grades will suffer. Dad's been real serious about me keeping up my grades."

"I'm sorry too, Matt," Robyn responded. "Actually, I'm disappointed. You were—are—a good leader."

"Hey," Matt said a little defensively, "it's not like I've dropped out or become a doper or something. I'm still in my Sunday school class, and I'll even still be there on Wednesday nights. Most of the time, anyway."

"I know. I'm not trying to make you feel guilty," she said. "We'll survive. And we'll support you. I'll see that the whole gang is at your first home meet. Okay?"

"Sure. Thanks."

In the weeks ahead, Matt threw himself into running. Sometimes he lost track of the day, and all he could remember was the endless cross country course ahead of him. Matt would start sooner and stay later than even Coach Dallas, who marveled at his endurance.

Nearly half a dozen meets later, Matt lay in his bed finishing his homework. Where had the day gone? In fact, where had the months gone? Matt thought, panic-stricken. He quickly dialed Martin's number.

"Yo, Martin. What's happenin'?"

"Nothing. Conjugating French verbs. Wanna know how to say 'That's a lovely Cadillac you've got sticking out of your nose' in French?"

"Some other time. Right now I just need to take a breather. It seems all I'm doing is cross country and homework. I don't even get to see Gaile on Saturdays much because I'm too tired after the meets. Sometimes I wonder, why am I doing this stuff anyway?"

"Good question, big guy. I dunno. Prestige? Enjoyment? To stay in shape for football? For the women? Money?"

"Aw, be serious, Martin. I mean, I've had to give up the

youth group. I don't see Dad or Gaile much. I look a lot better—
I've put on some muscle. But I'm tired all the time. I just don't
know what the Lord wants me to do. Am I running for fun or
prestige?"

Martin thought quietly for a moment. "Pal, you're on your
own with that one. No one can answer that but you."

What would you do?

*If Matt decides he's running for prestige and glory, turn to
page 95.*
If he's running for enjoyment, turn to page 102.

This was the first time Matt had been this close to Genie. And he liked it. He liked Wanda acting jealous. He liked the suggestive things Therese was saying, even if she was tipsy.

He also knew that—before tonight—Genie had barely paid any attention to him. Ever.

Am I a different guy than I was yesterday? he thought. Nope. Same me. The only difference is that as of today I'm on varsity. Big deal.

But oh! Genie's eyes. They were hazel with flecks of gold. He'd never been close enough to notice before.

But what about Gaile? Gaile had been his girlfriend for the past year. She'd liked him when he was a nobody on the junior varsity. She liked him now.

But Genie was here. Now.

Matt steered the conversation away from himself. He talked to the girls and laughed to himself as they jockeyed for position.

"Genie, don't you think you should check on James?" Soozi purred.

"James is a big boy, and it's not like we're going steady or anything," Genie said, her eyes flashing. She turned back to Matt. "Besides, it's nice to talk to somebody with something in his head besides hormones."

The circle of girls around Matt grew. He was enjoying himself, but he made sure everybody felt included. He flirted with a heavyset girl who stood at the back. He made Wanda tell about the time she'd won district in the prose-reading contest. He tried not to think of Genie's perfume, so close.

At last, Matt excused himself. "I've gotta visit the boy's room," he mumbled. "I'll be back in a minute." In the bathroom, he realized he'd forgotten the tub was the cooler for the beer. But before he could leave, he smelled Genie's perfume again.

"Matt, I hope you don't think I'm too ... forward," Genie said. "But you know, there's nothing between James and me. We ... we broke up. He's with Rhonda."

Matt's head swam from the smell. Oh, but she was beautiful. She was the sexiest girl he'd ever known. She was ... so close.

"I was hoping you'd be here tonight, Matt," she continued. "I think we need to talk." Genie rested her hand on Matt's. "Can we go outside? It's so loud and ... public ... in here. Just for a little while?" Her golden-hazel eyes promised much.

Matt held an ice cube to his brow. Hooo boy! What a
night—and it had only just begun!

What would you do?

If Matt accepts Genie's invitation, turn to page 80.
If Matt cuts off Genie's move, turn to page 105.

Matt kept staring at the petition in his hands. "C'mon Brand, we haven't got all day!" Coach Charles barked.

Impulsively, Matt stood up and raised a hand. "Yes, Matt," the school board president said.

"Sir, I don't use steroids. But I just can't support mandatory drug testing." Matt's heart was pounding. "I don't know what the school district's lawyer says, but haven't other tests like this one faced some heavy-duty legal challenges? It seems to me like we're implying everybody's guilty until proven innocent. I'm sorry. I won't sign this list."

Matt's impromptu speech prompted cheers from the other players—including the ones who'd been using steroids.

The school board president looked sadly at Matt. "I'm sorry too, son. I expected something better from you."

That night at the youth group meeting, Matt tried to get the other members to support his stand. No one did, save Martin and Gaile.

A week later, the results of the first tests came back. Nearly half the team tested positive for steroids, including Martin.

Dee Dee found Matt immediately. "My dad checked on what you'd said, and you were right! Mandatory tests have been challenged in several school districts. Dad's lawyer said if the rest of the team joins us, we can get a temporary injunction against the school district that'll keep them from suspending any players until after a judge can hear the case—and that could take weeks!"

"Has everyone joined?" Matt asked.

"Everyone but Vernon," Dee Dee said with a hint of disgust in his voice. "That 'holy roller' thinks the guys who were caught ought to accept their punishment. Well, Vernon doesn't have to face Kirbyville's linemen with an offense made up of second teamers and JV players!"

"So Brand, what'll it be? You with us or not?"

What would you do?

If Matt accepts the test results and consequences, turn to page 56.
If he joins a legal challenge to the testing, turn to page 71.

"No thanks, Dee Dee," Matt said finally. "That's not for me."

Dee Dee grunted and walked away. But Matt felt good about his decision. He thought Jesus would've done the same thing.

■

Matt and Martin sat in the Dairy Barn, nursing chocolate peanut butter malts. Martin's suspension from the football team hit them both hard.

"Matt, I want you to do something for me," Martin said. "I need your help making sure no one ever makes my mistake again."

"How can we do that?"

"We've gotta educate kids. We've gotta tell them what steroids do to your body—and your mind. We've gotta tell them about the dangers of long-term use. We've gotta tell them the penalties you could face for taking steroids."

"Martin, you're a better man than I am," Matt said. "If I'd been in your cleats, I'd be blaming God. I'll get on it tonight."

Matt was true to his word. He rallied the Christian athletes' fellowship. They studied anabolic steroids from every angle. They sent off for materials. They invited sports-medicine doctors—as well as professional and college athletes—to speak at the school. They held rallies and seminars.

The final rally took place during lunch on the last day of school. Matt recapped the latest findings from the Yale University School of Medicine. The report stated that steroid users eventually craved the hormones much the way cocaine addicts crave crack. He reported on a new British study that showed that steroids only had a marginal impact on a subject's muscle mass—that most of the changes were mental, not physical. And he gave an emotional appeal urging all the students to unite in signing a drug-free pact.

When he was finished, silence spread across the auditorium.

Just when Matt despaired of having embarrassed himself for life, Dee Dee silently stood. Across the aisle, after a moment of hesitation, Gaile stood too. Then Genie Salat. Followed by most of the baseball team and the band—and on it went until everyone in the audience was standing and applauding. It was great!

With tears in his eyes, Matt walked into the audience and found Martin. As they embraced, the other students came pouring out of their seats to congratulate Matt and sign the pacts.

"It was worth it, Matt," Martin whispered. "This makes it all worth it. You did it!"

"Thank you, God," Matt said, the tears flowing down his cheeks. "Thank you for everything."

The End

In the days following The Studebaker's talk, Matt found himself more and more attracted to basketball.

"Are you crazy?" Martin yelled when Matt told him he was going out for the team. "You haven't played since eighth grade. And even if you made it, you'd have to see Coach Trail every day. Are you sure you're up to that?"

Coach Trail, overweight and always angry, was the line coach for the football team. He coached the basketball team only because it meant extra money. What little he knew about basketball came out of outdated basketball textbooks. Worse than that, his temper was legendary.

"I know, I know," Matt said, "but I've been playing on weekends, and it really feels good. Besides, the best players all graduated last year. I might even get to start!"

Much to his delight, Matt did make the varsity. But Trail had gotten worse—not better—with age. He used every form of cheating and intimidation conceivable. With each incident, the knot in Matt's stomach twisted tighter.

But all of the tricks in the world couldn't overcome a lack of talent—or coaching ability. Matt's team got beat regularly. Trail hurled abuse on the officials, the other teams and, especially, his own players. One by one players quit the team, dreading the bus rides back from rival courts.

"I can't stand it any longer," Matt told his father. "My stomach hurts all the time."

"Sounds like Trail's pretty obsessed with winning," his father mused. "Why do the school officials tolerate him?"

"Aw, because he's available, and he's Coach Charles' best friend. Gee, Trail as a guy's best friend ... That gives me the shivers!"

"So, what are you going to do?"

"If I quit, he'll make it rough on me if I try out for football next year," Matt said. "But I never really thought about what it'd be like to play for someone who believes in winning at any cost. Nothing's worth that."

"I agree, son. I don't like what I see or hear from the stands."

"You know, Dad," Matt continued. "I also realized while sitting there gathering splinters on the bench that what I've really wanted to do all along was play football."

"That won't be easy, Matt. Not only will you have Trail to

contend with, you'll be a year behind the rest of the guys. You up for it?"

"You bet!" Matt said. "I'll always wonder if I was good enough if I don't try."

■

Matt quit basketball, then convinced Martin to train with him for football tryouts in the fall. And they trained virtually every day—running, lifting weights, skipping rope, even hiking.

When two-a-days began on August 15th, Matt and Martin were at the field stretching at 6 a.m. The coaches hardly recognized either guy. They'd both put on a lot of muscle.

"Well, well, what do we have here?" Coach Charles asked. "Looks like we've got a couple of eager beavers. Well, we'll see if you've got what it takes to make it this time."

Blind choice:

Without looking ahead, turn to page 24 or page 43 to see if Matt makes the team.

"I can't do it, Coach," Matt said. "The youth group needs me. I can see how much time cross country would take. Honestly, Coach, would there be any time left after committing to cross country?"

Dallas mused a moment. "Either cross country is important to you, or it's not, Matt. You'll run nearly every day until dark. You'll be gone all day Saturday at meets. And when you get back, you'll be too tired to do anything but veg out. Honest enough?"

"Thanks, Coach. You deserve better than me giving you one day's worth of running. And I should've checked all this out before I tried out today," Matt said.

They walked into the dressing room.

"Hey, you running with us or what?" one of the seniors called out as they passed by.

Matt stopped and turned to the other runners. "I screwed up guys. I had no idea the time you put into cross country."

"So, ol' Mattie-boy's wimping out on us," the senior said. "Can't cut it with the football team, so he's gonna grace us lowly runners with his presence. Then when he sees that this is where the *real* men are, he cops out. Nice job, Brand. I never figured you for a quitter."

"That's enough, Greenwood," Dallas shot back. "Matt made a mistake. Day comes when you make a mistake, I hope you're man enough to admit it too."

■

Later, Martin dropped by the field house to see how things went. He found Matt sitting alone inside. Matt recounted the afternoon's events to his friend.

"Great buncha guys, sorry I had to do them dirty," Matt said.

"Okay, so cross country didn't work out. What else do you want to do?"

"I guess ... I guess I *really* want to play football next year. I'd love to make the team before I graduate."

"Okay, great! Me too! So let's make a pact right now," Martin said. "You an' me. We'll work out every day. Rain or shine. No matter what else is going on. We'll hit the weights here in the field house after the football team is out on the field, and we'll run every day after that."

"You're serious, aren't you?" Matt said.

"You bet I'm serious. This is what I wanted to do all along. We'll work it around church and school and social schedules, but we'll bust it every day of the year. And come two-a-days next summer, we'll be in awesome shape. You with me?"

"You know it, compadre!"

Matt and Martin kept their vow. They trained virtually every day. They ran through hail and heat waves. They pumped iron 'til the coaches ran them out of the field house. They skipped rope, gave up soft drinks and candy, and went on hikes deep into the woods around the school. And they rarely missed a service at church. Both boys spent time in prayer and studying the Word. They were getting their spiritual lives in shape along with their bodies.

When two-a-days began on August 15th, Matt and Martin were at the field stretching at 6 a.m. When the coaches arrived, they hardly recognized either Matt or Martin. They'd both put on a lot of muscle.

"Well, well, what do we have here?" Coach Charles asked. "Looks like we've got a couple of eager beavers. Well, we'll see if you've got what it takes to make it this time."

Blind choice:

Without looking ahead, turn to page 24 or page 43 to continue the story.

The next day at the stadium, passing motorists noticed Coach Charles screaming at a bunch of guys running up and down the bleachers.

"C'mon boys, only 18 to go," Coach Charles yelled. "Pick it up now! No lollygagging!"

Matt shifted his shoulder pads to a more comfortable position as he trudged up the bleachers again. They'd only been at this since 8 a.m., but he was dripping with sweat. If only his head didn't pound so much. It must be the beer.

On the way down, one of his cleats caught, and he pitched forward. He had enough presence of mind to protect his hands but still landed hard on his helmet and shoulders, skinning his forearm.

"Up and at 'em, Brand," Charles shouted. "You wanna rest, you do it on your time, not mine."

As Saturday morning wore on, the rest of the team showed up for the regular "optional" stretching and agility drills. By now Matt and the other partygoers were staggering around the track, carrying tackling dummies on their shoulders.

"Nice going rookie!" one player shouted to Matt, "welcome to the NFL!"

"Yeah, guys," another chimed in, "wouldn't a nice cold one taste good right now?"

Soon most of the other players were running circles around the partygoers as they struggled just to put one foot in front of the other. Whenever Matt faltered or slowed down, the other players screamed at him to continue, to put more effort into it. But they didn't say much to Dee Dee, James or Bink—they knew better.

Lord, give me strength not to say anything, Matt prayed through a haze of pain.

By noon, Coach Charles was bored with humiliating the guys and told them to leave. But in the week ahead, he mercilessly ragged on Matt and the other partygoers. Nothing they did was good enough. Supported only by Martin, Matt worked twice as hard in practice.

Playing with the second team as weakside linebacker, his hits were savage—but clean. As second-team quarterback, he took a host of late hits right in front of Coach Charles but always bounced up, cheering his team on. Gradually, it wasn't as much fun to dump on Matt. By Friday, the pressure had eased.

Then game day arrived. The Center Panthers were a tough defensive team. In the first half, the Eagles and Panthers traded hard-earned field goals. Matt was the only player who hadn't seen action. In the locker room at halftime, Charles changed the offense. Instead of straight-ahead power plays and sweeps, he switched to more option plays, misdirection plays and traps.

Opening the second half, the Eagles moved down the field. At the Panther 44, Dee Dee called a triple option. The safety didn't bite. When Dee Dee tried to turn upfield, the safety nailed him on the hip. Dee Dee managed to hold on to the ball, but lay writhing in pain on the grass.

Charles cursed, then looked at Matt.

"Okay, rook, you're in. Don't embarrass me."

Matt hopped up and ran onto the field. As he headed toward the huddle, his mind raced. This is my big chance, he thought. A chance to redeem myself. Oh, God, don't let me blow it!

Blind choice:

Without looking ahead, turn to page 34 or page 37 to continue the story.

Matt ran into Bink and James in the hall. "Hey, did you guys see this stupid article in the Echo?" Matt asked.

"Yup, sure did," James said. "Buncha sissies. People who can't play football write about it."

"Yeah," said Bink, " 'sides, we still got one more chance to win district this week against Kirbyville. You can't let those other players take advantage of you or they'll never let up. It wasn't your fault."

"That's right," Matt said, encouraged by their response. "Wasn't nothin' I could do. Hey, nobody's perfect."

The Kirbyville Wildcats were the Eagle's big rival, and the winner would represent the district in the play-offs. The game turned into a high-scoring affair, filled with big plays and impressive drives. Matt and James grew frustrated trying to slow down the Kirbyville offense.

To make matters worse, some of the Wildcats were needling Matt, trying to pick a fight. They'd seen the films of the Buna game, and knew he could get rattled.

Matt held his temper until the waning moments of the fourth quarter when the Eagles held a 10-point lead. A Wildcat tackle hit him late after a play, and Matt exploded. He whipped off his helmet and began beating the player with it. Both benches emptied, and Matt again was thrown out of the game. Kirbyville scored again, but time expired before the Wildcats could get the football back. The Eagles won 36 to 33.

Monday after school, the Christian athletes organization met at First Church, and several players questioned Matt about his behavior.

"It just doesn't look right for a Christian to be fighting all the time," Vernon said. "I mean, come on Matt! You're head of your youth group! Use your head, man!"

Other players agreed.

"Hey, if the coaches didn't like it, they'd tell me," Matt responded. "You weren't out there. You don't know the dirty things the Wildcats were doing to me, the stuff they were sayin'. You wouldn't have stood for it either, Vernon!"

"I *was* out there, Matt," Vernon said. "They said the same things to everybody. You're just the only one they knew they could get to."

In desperation, Matt turned to Coach Mills. "Coach, you tell them. I didn't have any choice, did I? Tell them!"

"I'm not speaking as your coach now, Matt," Mills said, "I'm speaking as a Christian brother." He paused. "The truth is you're a Christian, a 'little Christ.' Christ is supposed to live in you all the time. In church, on the football field, everywhere. You're his representative. People judge other Christians and the church by how you behave, especially since you hold a leadership role at First Church.

Matt clenched his fists unconsciously.

"And as for your question, I believe the answer is yes." Mills continued, "You *did* have a choice. Every fight takes two people. Coach Dallas and I don't agree with the other coaches when it comes to your play. And we've told them so. Winning just isn't worth it."

Nearly blinded by angry tears, Matt stormed from the room.

■

The victory over Kirbyville meant the Eagles faced Crockett in bi-district. Again, Matt's reputation preceded him. Some of the Crockett players made insulting comments, hoping to goad Matt into another fight.

Early in the second half, Matt suffered an illegal crack-back block from the burly Crockett fullback. The referee didn't see the foul. Matt bounced up, wincing in pain, his fists doubled. The fullback stood his ground and threatened Matt under his breath.

What would you do?

If Matt starts another fight, turn to page 9.
If he stays calm, turn to page 19.

Late that night, Matt called Martin. "You asleep?"

"Not anymore," Martin mumbled. "What's the matter?"

"Well," Matt said. "I've been praying about it all evening. If we don't take a stand for what we believe now, it'll only get worse. So what'll we do next?"

"Well, after a good night's sleep, I suggest we check first with the principal, then with Coach Mills about what we *can* do. There's something about this church-and-state stuff that won't allow us to have prayer meetings on campus or something," Martin said, stifling a yawn.

"Good thinking!" Matt said. "I'll meet you at the principal's office first thing in the morning."

■

Martin was right. The high school wouldn't allow religious meetings of any kind in school buildings during school hours, but the principal was all for some kind of Christian athletes' group—providing it had a sponsor.

At the field house, Coaches Mills and Dallas both agreed to be sponsors. Both had been members of Fellowship of Christian Athletes while in college.

Early meetings—held in the weight room—weren't impressive. Only four other students showed up—two from the football team. But Matt and Martin kept plugging away. Bink and James made Matt's and Martin's lives miserable in the locker room, calling them "fanatics" and "holy Joes." But more and more of the football players came to their lunch time get-togethers and pre-game prayer meetings.

■

The Kountze Kangaroos gave the Eagles fits. The tackling was brutal and several players were injured. Matt didn't play at quarterback, but had worked his way up to the second-team weakside linebacker. When the starter went down with a knee injury, Matt stepped in and delivered several vicious hits on 'Roo runners. Each time, he helped the player up and darted back to the defensive huddle.

Dee Dee missed a long field goal in the game's closing moments. Then on the 'Roo's last play, the 'Roo's quarterback tried a desperation pass toward the goal line. A Kountze player caught

the ball and dove for the end zone, but was hit head-on by Matt.
The force of the blow shook the stadium, and gasps went up from
the crowd. Matt shook the cobwebs from his head and bounded
to where the 'Roo player lay stunned on the two-yard line. The
receiver was shaken by the hit but unharmed. The game ended in
a 14 to 14 tie.

In the locker room, Dee Dee limped over to Matt.

"Nice hit on that last play, rook," Dee Dee said. "You saved
the game for me. You really leveled that guy."

Matt smiled, too tired to respond. He barely had strength to
pull off his helmet.

Dee Dee continued, "Uh, Matt, this'll probably sound like a
dumb question, but I gotta ask it anyway. You were a hittin' ma-
chine out there. If you were faster, you'd be starting. As it was,
you really clobbered some of those guys. It was all clean and fair,
don't get me wrong. But you cleaned their clocks.

"Here's my question: You're a member of this Christian athlete's club. You're even head of the youth group at First Church,
right? So how does somebody who's a Christian deliver hits like
that? I mean, doesn't the Bible say something about turning the
other cheek and stuff?"

Matt squirmed. These guys have been laughing at me all
year, he thought. Why give them ammunition now? How can I
respond to a question like that?

What would you do?

If Matt sidesteps the question, turn to page 90.
If he uses the chance to share his faith, turn to page 118.

Matt and James stared at each other. If I'm going to lead these guys someday, they have to respect me, Matt thought. If I back down, they'll never take me seriously. It all comes down to this.

"Sure. Why not? You're on, James." Matt decided to take the offensive. "So, care to put a little something on this? A friendly wager, perhaps?"

James was dumbfounded. The fool had called his bluff. "Uh, yeah. Okay, 10 bucks says you can't do it, rook."

"Done." Matt grabbed the six-pack, then carelessly tossed it back. "Hey, if I'm gonna chug six of these babies, I better make it a lite beer! Coach wouldn't like it if I started waddling around the field!" The onlookers roared their approval.

Matt grew bolder, fueled by the crowd's response. Hey, he thought, this ain't bad. Maybe if I do it just this once, I'll never have to do something like this again. But even as he smiled at Genie, Matt knew he was putting aside what he believed just to make a good impression on people he barely knew.

Matt tried to act casual as he grabbed a six-pack of lite beer and flipped the top on one. He threw back his head and drank half the can in a single gulp. Oh well, here goes, he thought half-sadly. Let's get it done. The beer tasted like carbonated vinegar. He stopped, wiped his mouth, winked at the crowd and finished it off. The other players began chanting. "Go! Go! Go!"

Matt finished the second can nearly as quickly. The cold from the beer gave him a headache. He passed the empty can to James, who crushed it. Matt began drinking a third can, only a little slower than the first two.

Perhaps it was the chanting of the football players, perhaps the beer had already made Matt lightheaded—but no one heard Coach Charles come in. And, until he was standing a couple of feet from Matt, no one saw him either.

In a heartbeat, the room became deathly still. The silence startled Matt, and he choked a little on his beer. When he looked up, Coach Charles was standing in front of him.

"Oh, hi Coach!" Matt said, his tongue thick. "Can I get you something to drink?"

Blind choice:

Without looking ahead, turn to page 30 or page 62 to see how the coach will react.

After a little thought, Matt decided he could get to know the athletes without playing sports. But it wasn't easy. Some were suspicious; others simply didn't have the time.

To help bridge the gap, Matt began attending meets and games. Sometimes it meant studying in the car or between quarters. Matt tried to attend every girls' volleyball game, every track meet, every swim meet, as well as all the "major" sports.

Over time, Matt learned about all the sports and began writing them up for the school newspaper (which meant he attended even more games). It was fun, and the athletes—particularly those in the lesser-attended sports—appreciated his time and effort.

Eagle athletes grew accustomed to seeing Matt in the stands cheering them on. At the end of his junior year, the athletes voted him "Fan of the Year" at the high school All-Sports Banquet.

Matt continued supporting the athletes throughout his senior year as well. Between church, school and sporting events, he never again tried out for any of the teams. But he hardly missed being an athlete.

One spring day while he sat with Gaile in the stands at a baseball game against Kirbyville, she asked him if he ever missed playing.

Matt paused a moment and shaded his eyes against the bright Texas sun.

"No, I guess not," he replied. "I had a lot of pride, and playing football fed that pride. Plus, I've learned more about people by going to all these games. I think I've learned more about discipline and sacrifice from watching people put in the hours for swimming or volleyball than I actually learned from playing football."

"I don't doubt it," Gaile said jokingly. Matt smiled.

"There's a verse that Robyn told me back when I was a junior that has helped me a lot. I think it's 1 Corinthians 9:25. The first part says something like, um, everyone who competes in a game goes into strict training, but they do it to get a crown that doesn't last.

"Sports are great, but I get too caught up in them. The way I figure it, I'm better off putting my effort into a crown that lasts forever. I want to serve God."

"Now, that's what I've been waiting to hear," Gaile said with a sly smile.

The End

Matt decided to join the lawsuit against the testing procedure. Distracted by the legal proceedings, the Eagles played erratically as the season wore on, often just well enough to win.

At last, the judge ruled that while drug testing didn't violate any civil rights, this particular test was administered unfairly. Additionally, the judge said new tests couldn't be given until a fair and equitable system for testing was devised—a system the judge would have to approve in advance. In the meantime, all the players who'd tested positive the first time could play.

Matt volunteered to serve as the student body representative on the committee to establish uniform testing procedures.

As the season wore on, the Eagles were still in the hunt for a district title. A late-season game with the Center Panthers was pivotal. It proved to be a hard-fought defensive struggle.

At the start of the second half, Dee Dee tried a triple-option play around the right end. The Panther safety didn't bite and nailed him on the hip. Dee Dee fell to the turf, writhing in pain.

Coach Charles threw down his clipboard, then looked up and down the sidelines. "Brand! Where are you, boy? Get in there!"

Startled, Matt pulled on his helmet and started to run out on the field. Martin grabbed his jersey as he passed.

"You can do it—go get 'em!"

Matt's mind raced as he ran onto the field. This is my big shot, he thought. I've gotta make this look good. God, please don't let me blow it!

Blind choice:

Without looking ahead, turn to page 34 or page 37 to continue the story.

Coach Dallas sat by Matt on the long bus ride home.

Gaile, Martin and Dad took turns sitting with him through Sunday.

Robyn came by after school.

With each person who spent time with him, Matt's doubts about his self-worth without cross country seemed to fade a little more. With each visitor who came because he needed help, he saw it wasn't his success in cross country that mattered to these people. Matt Brand mattered.

Equipped with crutches, Matt hobbled around the campus for a few days. At first he was something of a celebrity, and every-one—including the cheerleaders—signed his cast. Later in the week, when the newness wore off, no one made a big deal about it anymore.

His skin itched under the cast. He wanted to take a shower without worrying about getting the cast wet. His toes were cold sticking out of the cast. But he survived.

■

One day, just before Christmas break, Coach Dallas was startled by a knock on his door late one evening. It was Matt, Gaile and Martin.

"We wanted to sing some Christmas carols," Matt explained, "but the only one we all knew was 'Jingle Bells.' "

"Come in, come in," Dallas said. "To what do I owe this honor?"

"I just wanted to say thanks, Coach," Matt said. "Remember that stuff you told me on the bus to Hardin-Bush? You know, about me putting cross country first in my life?"

"Mmm, I think so," Dallas said, "but I don't remember want-ing you to break your ankle."

"Maybe that's the only way God could get my attention," Matt said. "If it wasn't for you and Gaile and Martin and Robyn McGregor down at First Church, I don't know what would've become of me. I know all of you prayed for me and stuff, and ... and I don't know how to thank you."

Coach Dallas looked embarrassed and shook his head.

"Coach, I've tried to tell all of them thank you. I wanted to tell you too. If my ankle heals by next year, I'll be back out. If not, I'll work as your assistant or trainer or something.

"Whatever happens, I want you to know I'm trying to put my life into perspective. I'm gonna really put God back first in my life. I guess that sounds dumb, but I really mean it. You helped more than you'll ever know.

"Merry Christmas, Coach," Matt said as his friends helped him out the door.

"Merry Christmas to you too," Coach Dallas responded. "You couldn't possibly have given me a better Christmas present."

The End

After football practice, Matt took the newspaper to his youth minister, Robyn McGregor, who read it in her office.

"What do you think?" he asked.

"What do *you* think?" she responded.

"I don't know," Matt said. "I guess I wonder if what they're saying is true."

Robyn leaned back in her chair. "Are you having trouble controlling your temper?"

"Yeah, sometimes." Matt looked at his shoe for no reason.

"I could quote you a whole bunch of scripture on anger," Robyn said, "but I suspect you know them already. Obviously, God isn't real wild about selfish anger."

She grabbed her Bible. "Listen. Here's one verse to remember the next time someone tries to pick a fight: 'No temptation has seized you except what is common to man. And God is faithful; he will not let you be tempted beyond what you can bear. But when you are tempted, he will also provide a way out so that you can stand up under it.' That's 1 Corinthians 10:13."

"Hmm," Matt mused. "I guess this comes under the broad category of 'Turn the other cheek.' "

"In a way," she said. "Don't give them an excuse. And if you're provoked—and it looks like you're going to be from now on—forgive them and walk away. That's what Jesus would do, I think. Make sense?"

"You always make sense, Robyn," Matt said.

■

The Kirbyville Wildcats played a wide-open offense, and the game became a high-scoring affair. Several players needled Matt, but no matter what they said or did, he forgave them and walked away.

Late in the game with the Eagles up by 10, Matt was in on a tackle with several teammates. After the play had been whistled dead, a Wildcat tight end rammed Matt in his lower back with his helmet. Matt cried out in pain and whirled around. The tight end stood there taunting him, urging him to fight, calling him names.

What would you do?

If Matt fights, turn to page 9.
If he stays calm, turn to page 19.

Matt's temper grew hotter and hotter the farther he walked with Martin away from the field house.

"Know what the kicker is? You know what really sticks in my craw?" Matt shouted. "Charles! Coach Charles. He wanted Ky all along."

"What makes you say that?"

"Aw, c'mon Martin. You saw the things Charles did to me during two-a-days. Calling me 'church boy.' Chewing me out when I hadn't done anything wrong. And yesterday when we finally made a good play, he made a point to say something nice to Sammy on his run, ignored me, then purposely made Lively mad at me by making him run the stands on my account!"

"Whatever you say, Matt," Martin sighed. "But hey, remember—I didn't make the team either. And I'm not ready to rip the coach limb from limb."

Matt rolled his eyes. But you weren't trying out for quarterback either, he thought.

■

In frustration, Matt decided to go see Robyn, his youth minister. He had some anger to vent, and she was always a good listener.

Robyn McGregor's office was the old custodian's closet. It was big enough for a desk, two chairs and a filing cabinet, but that was about all. Robyn sat and listened as Matt spewed out his pain and frustration, particularly at Coach Charles.

"The man's sick, sick, sick, Robyn. He *likes* hurting kids. He's run dumb ol' Sammy so many times up and down the stands he's got gashes on his shins that've never healed. There's something wrong about him, something evil. And it's not just me that thinks so either. Some of the other guys think so too."

"That's all pretty disturbing, Matt. You don't think any of the guys you talked to ever told Mr. Charles what you think of him?"

"No way! Those are my friends! They wouldn't betray me like that." Matt's stomach tightened. "At least, they better not have!" he added.

"Well, never mind that. If everything you say is true—and I have no reason to doubt you—do you think it's a good idea to talk about someone like that? Do you think it'll accomplish anything?"

"Yeah, sure it will. If enough guys agree, and we stick together, we can get our parents involved. Maybe the school board would investigate him."

Robyn spoke quietly. "Do you think most players think the same way you do?"

Matt thought for a moment, then shook his head.

"Half the players?" Robyn persisted. "Just a few?"

"Well, you see, the guys who're starting would never say anything bad about Coach Charles. They could get kicked off the team for causing trouble."

Robyn didn't say anything but continued to watch Matt.

"And the other guys, well, they've got to be careful too. He might never give them a chance."

"I see. Matt, let me ask it another way. Do you think it's a good idea for Christians to accuse others without first examining themselves? Is that what Jesus would've done?"

"You don't understand, Robyn. Charles had it in for me from the beginning! Besides, Jesus never met anyone like Coach Charles."

"Maybe not, but he died for people like Coach Charles. And Matt Brand. And Robyn McGregor."

Matt couldn't believe what he was hearing. He'd come to Robyn for comfort, and here he was getting lectured on being Christlike! He stared at her. He knew Robyn was right, but that didn't ease his anger.

At the same time, he thought, what does she know about football, about what it means to a guy? Maybe I should just be mad for a few days. Get it out of my system. Maybe it'll make me feel better.

What would you do?

If Matt accepts what Robyn is saying, turn to page 20.
If Matt blows Robyn off, turn to page 32.

▼

Matt decided to take the quiet approach. He wouldn't say or do anything to compromise his witness—not again. And he and Martin agreed that if anyone showed an interest in God or Christianity, both guys would follow up on it. They'd lead by example.

The only trouble was that nobody was following.

In fact, Matt wasn't sure anybody even noticed his new stance. The guys still talked trash, Coach Charles still swore, and when they mentioned something that happened at church, most of the other guys laughed.

Still, both were slowly, grudgingly accepted as full-fledged team members. Matt knew that acceptance was tentative, and he sure didn't want to do anything to alienate himself from the other guys.

"After all," he confided to Martin, "I'm just one step away from being the starting quarterback. I've got to be able to lead these guys once I step out on the field. I can't lead if they don't trust me. Or if I'm not one of them."

Martin said nothing.

Because the school was small, Matt had also worked his way up to second-team weakside linebacker—even though he wasn't fast enough or strong enough to be a starter on defense. After most practices he was so tired he could barely move.

One day still early in the season, while Matt and Martin were talking in the locker room after practice, Bink and James came up. James popped Matt's bare back with a wet towel. Matt howled and jumped up to confront his tormenter.

"You're a big, tough guy in front of all the coaches, ain'cha rookie?" James sneered. "How come you weren't that tough with the dudes from Newton? I've never seen you challenge one player after a dirty hit." James turned his back and walked off.

Bink came over and pulled Matt down next to him.

"Don't pay any attention to him," he told Matt. "He's just worried. Vernon just told Coach his knee's been bothering him. Something happens to Vernon, and you take his place."

Matt froze. Vernon was the starting weakside linebacker. A ferocious hitter, Vernon frequently disregarded personal safety to break up plays. Matt knew he wasn't in Vernon's league.

"Coach would never tell you this, but you're too small to handle some of the big guys from Kirbyville or Center, Matt. They'll beat you like an old rag doll."

Matt started to protest, but Bink cut him off.

"Hey, I didn't come over here to criticize you. I'm just here to help you out." Bink dropped his voice to a whisper and pulled something out of his pocket.

Matt looked at the small bottle of pills in Bink's hand.

" 'Roids, Matt. They'll beef you up in no time. Look at this." Bink pulled off his shirt and flexed his chest and arm muscles. They rippled like a wheat field on a windy Kansas day. "That's just from taking them for a few months."

Matt's head reeled. Steroids! He remembered a study that showed that people who pump up using anabolic steroids may become addicted and crave them—like any other drug.

"But, aren't they illegal or something?" he sputtered.

"Naw, not really," Bink said as he pulled his shirt back on. "Besides, there's a booster here in town who's paying for them. All you gotta do is go over to Johnny Watson's. Tell him I sent you. Johnny knows all about these things. He's like an expert."

Matt hesitated. He knew the steroids would help bulk up his puny muscles—but at what cost? Suddenly, he was aware of the whole locker room watching him. Even James stood off to one side. Matt could see Vernon sitting with his knee in the whirlpool, his face contorted with pain. Could he let the whole team down? Could he let himself down? Should he?

What would you do?

If Matt accepts the steroids, turn to page 82.
If he turns down Bink's offer, turn to page 88.

Outside under the willow, Matt kissed Genie on the cheek. He buried his face in her hair and held her so tightly his arms ached. When she kissed him, he felt his heart would pound right out of his chest.

∎

That was the beginning of a dizzying courtship. Matt and Genie became inseparable. Every post-game party, every dance, every movie, on the phone every night. Matt ran in circles he'd only watched from afar before. Genie was the most popular girl in school. She knew everybody. Everywhere she went, a crowd of girls clustered around her like chicks around a mother hen.

Matt's status shot up. If he wore mismatched socks to school, the next day half the guys at school wore mismatched socks. When he walked into the lunchroom, there were always several guys calling for him to sit with them.

The only place things weren't so good was at church. Gaile gracefully bowed out of the picture. No scene, no argument, no crying—just plenty of loss and betrayal in her eyes. Martin was still around. But Matt spent most of his time with Genie, so he only saw Martin at practice. And Martin seemed distant too.

Then one Sunday morning, Matt sat alone in church—perhaps for the first time in his life. The night before, he and Genie had held court at the Country Club—at a dance in honor of Genie's birthday. He'd been big stuff then. What was different now? It was like he was a leper or something. Aw, Matt thought, they're just jealous. Who needs them?

He sang the next hymn alone.

I do, he thought sadly.

After church, he asked Martin if they could talk. They sat in Martin's car, where in the past they'd sat for hours talking about anything and everything. Martin could see the turmoil in Matt's face.

Matt tried to think objectively. What did he and Genie talk about? What so-and-so wore, who was with who, where the party was tonight.

What did he and Gaile use to talk about? Events, not things. Humanity, not other people. Eternal life, not endless parties.

Why was he dating Genie?

Long pause.

To be popular.

He looked up at Martin. "What am I going to do?"

Martin studied his friend. Matt was reaching out to him. Martin forgave him for a month of insensitive behavior, of ignoring his best friend, of snubbing the guy who'd stuck by him through thick and thin.

"What are your choices, Matt?"

"I can keep dating Genie. I can keep all the things I've always dreamed of—a beautiful cheerleader by my side, status, acceptance, excitement. All that stuff. The catch is, of course, that Genie's mine only as long as I'm the backup quarterback. That could change with one tackle."

"Too true," Martin said.

"Or I can admit I'm only dating her to be popular, and give it all up. And then I'll be worse off than I was before, because I won't even have Gaile. And I don't blame her."

"Matt," Martin said, "Gaile's not the only thing you've given up." There was no anger, no threat in Martin's voice. Only pain. "And only you can decide if being the most popular guy in school—for now—is worth it."

What would you do?

If Matt keeps dating Genie, turn to page 119.

If Matt breaks up with Genie, turn to page 12.

Matt couldn't shake the other guys' stares.

"So, what's it gonna be, rook?" Bink asked, this time with more urgency. "You gonna be a man and help out the team? Or you gonna be a mamma's boy?"

Matt took the bottle from Bink's hand.

"I knew you'd come through, Brand!" Bink pounded him on the back. "First thing we do is have a long talk with 'Uncle Johnny' Watson. He'll put all your fears to rest. Trust me."

■

Johnny and Bink were right. The steroids did help Matt beef up. Within weeks, even the coaches were noticing his new physique. Within a month, so did Genie Salat.

On the field, Matt's new-found muscle mass got him more and more playing time on defense. When Vernon sat out a game with an injury, Matt stepped in and performed well.

Matt's personality was changing as well. His temper heated up on the playing field and in practice, once even challenging James to a fight. The coaches seemed thrilled with his new, more aggressive nature. No one asked where it came from.

As the season passed the midpoint, Matt's workouts in the weight room and regular steroid use had helped him bulk up beyond his wildest dreams. Gradually, he rationalized away his qualms—even the religious ones—about drug use. Eventually he didn't think about them at all.

One night, after he'd finished his homework, Matt found himself staring at his body in the mirror. Who *is* that muscular dude? he wondered.

"Matt, sports are on," his father called from the living room. Matt pulled on a sweat shirt and plopped in front of the television, doing sit-ups as he watched.

"The sports world was saddened today by the loss of Glenn Overstreet, an All-Pro middle linebacker with Houston," the announcer said. Matt bolted up and listened. "Overstreet, known for his kamikaze attitude and fierce tackling, died earlier today from an apparent self-inflicted gunshot wound.

"Overstreet was under a three-game suspension for steroid use. He had been admitted into the NFL's drug rehabilitation program for assistance in breaking a dependency resulting from long-term anabolic steroid abuse."

Matt suddenly felt violently ill and began to sweat profusely.

"A doctor at the clinic reported that Overstreet had become despondent since being taken off steroids last month. Recent studies from the Yale University School of Medicine seem to confirm that steroids have an addictive nature—much like cocaine. Police are currently treating Overstreet's shooting as a suicide."

Matt switched off the television.

"Matt, is something wrong?" his father asked.

"No, nothing's wrong, everything's fine," Matt said. "I think I'll go to bed now, okay?"

"Sure, son," his father said as he watched Matt stumble out of the room.

Once in his room, Matt lay on his bed, staring at the ceiling. Matt's thoughts came so fast they were a blur. Overstreet was only 29 years old. He'd been using steroids nearly 15 years. Now he's dead.

I'll sure never take them 15 years. Should I quit now? What would the guys say? I mean, I'm just now getting good. Maybe I should wait until after football season. Until after my senior year? after college? Should I even quit? I mean, it's not like I'm addicted or anything. I could quit tomorrow if I wanted to.

Couldn't I?

What would you do?

If Matt continues using steroids, turn to page 17.
If he stops using steroids, turn to page 36.

Matt tried to be brave about his bad break, but his attitude got worse. Without sports, he floundered. He tried several hobbies but got bored with them. He read the sports pages avidly and immersed himself in the box scores and averages of his favorite teams. But nothing could replace athletics in his life.

The year passed slowly, and Matt never emerged from what Martin called his "blue funk." He was often moody and sometimes surly, and some of his friends drifted away.

At the beginning of summer after his ankle had healed, Matt realized he needed to get football out of his system—one way or another. After training on his own to get his strength up, he decided to go out for the varsity team again. As two-a-days approached, his training intensified—as did his spirits.

He couldn't read his progress during two-a-days. He was locked in a struggle with Ky for the starting quarterback job. Matt had the better arm, but Ky had stuck with the team and practiced with the receivers all through the spring and summer.

When the day came for Coach Charles to list the varsity roster, Matt had no idea where he stood.

Blind choice:

Without looking ahead, turn to page 104 or page 24 to continue the story.

Matt's answer came after several nights of prayer. "I've gotta give it a shot. I've gotta try out again," he told his dad. His dad just smiled.

Matt met with Coach Mills and Coach Dallas, and they helped him set up a training routine that would get him in shape to play football his senior year. He followed it religiously, even jogging during the cold and wet spring and pumping iron faithfully in the gym.

When two-a-days started in mid-August, Matt was ready. But he was worried about his skills. He hadn't played football in more than a year and a half, while Ky had worked out with the receivers during the off-season.

Some players remembered Matt's comments about "dumb jocks" and made practices even harder on him. He apologized to each one, then worked twice as hard as anyone else during two-a-days.

After the final afternoon workout of two-a-days, Coach Charles posted the starting roster on the bulletin board outside the field house. Matt waited until most of the other athletes had inspected the list before walking up to the board. He had no idea what to expect. Would he make the team or face disappointment again?

Blind choice:

Without looking ahead, turn to page 24 or page 43 to see if Matt makes the team.

Matt continued his workouts under Johnny Watson's watchful eye and got to where he enjoyed them again. But he was frustrated because he couldn't develop the muscles he saw on other players.

One day, Watson bought him a soft drink, and they sat on the steps to the gym.

"Matt, I gotta come clean with you here," Johnny said. "You probably aren't ever gonna have da muscles like Bink an' dem have. You don't got da right build or muscle structure."

"Yeah, I'd kinda figured that out by now, Johnny," Matt said.

"I've trained enough athletes to know a body type when I see one," Johnny continued. "I know what you could do well. Let me show you something."

Johnny drove Matt to the YMCA. Once inside, Johnny led Matt to an indoor swimming pool. The pool was heated and surrounded by glass—like a greenhouse.

"You ever do any swimming, son?" he asked.

"Oh yeah, I love it," Matt said. "I've even got my lifeguard training card. But I've always played football during swimming season. Except for now, I mean."

"Well, I t'ink you're gonna like this."

And he did.

With Johnny's help, Matt developed into a powerful swimmer. Soon he enjoyed it more than he'd ever enjoyed football. He liked the rhythmic, almost hypnotic nature of the sport, the feeling of self-reliance, the sense of being completely in shape. Matt often prayed during his hours in the pool, finding himself meditating after only a few laps.

As the school year ended, Matt was in the best shape of his life. Lean and trim, with strong muscles and enormous aerobic capacity. Just before his daily workout, he sat on the side of the pool and talked with Gaile, who'd also become an avid swimmer.

"Man, I'd love to try out for the swim team," he told her. "I think I could do well—I really do. But the swim team is kinda like the chess club, you know? It ... it just doesn't *mean* anything."

"You've never really gotten football out of your system, have you?" Gaile said. It was more of a statement than a question.

"No, I guess not," Matt replied. "Maybe I feel I've left some things undone in football. Maybe I need the prestige, the popularity that football brings. I dunno."

"It's an either/or thing, Matt," she said. "You swim, or you play football in the fall. I suppose it all comes back to why you're competing in the first place ... Have you prayed about it?"

"Yeah, a lot. All the time. And I think God's leading me to a decision. Do I do what I like best and stay a nobody? Or do I do what I like less and maybe, just maybe, be a somebody?"

What would you do?

If Matt goes out for the swim team, turn to page 98.
If he returns to football, turn to page 107.

Matt felt their eyes burn into him. "Bink, if you really cared about the team—like you always say you do—you wouldn't be trying to get people to damage their bodies with that junk."

Bink's eyes grew as wide as compact discs.

Matt continued, "Now, let me tell you something. I believe Christ lives in my body. I don't believe he wants us polluting it with dangerous chemicals. You do whatever you have to do: I won't squeal."

Matt walked over to the nearest weight station. "As for me, I'll bulk up ... *my* way. And don't worry. I won't let the team down when my time comes. I haven't yet."

Bink lunged at Matt, but the other players restrained him. "You better watch your back, Brand!" he screamed. "This isn't over—not by a long shot!"

■

Matt was the first to arrive and the last to leave the weights every day. In the weight room, he sometimes envied the bodies some of the other players were developing—seemingly overnight. But he compensated by working twice as hard.

Bink never spoke to him again, nor did many of the other seniors. That was fine with Matt. When they'd spoken before, it was usually to ridicule his faith.

One day late in the season, acting on a tip from a coach of a rival school, the school board voted to institute mandatory drug tests for all athletes. The decision shocked the players, including Matt. The school board president called for a meeting of all the football players in the auditorium.

"Gentlemen, we've been getting reports from other schools accusing the Eagles of steroid use," he said. "You can't imagine how this concerns—and embarrasses—me. I won't stand for this, and neither will members of the school board.

"Because of these charges, our school will implement manda-tory drug testing, beginning this week."

A general buzz that sounded like a chain saw ripped through the rows of students.

"I want each of you to support this decision both privately and publicly. We're passing around a sheet for each of you to sign indicating you're drug-free and that you support this program." The buzz erupted into an angry shout. Many players jumped up to challenge the legality of both the testing and the petition.

Matt heard something strange amid the hubbub and looked at Martin, who was sitting to his left. Martin was sniffling, tears streaking down his cheeks.

"Martin, not you!" Matt gasped. "When did you start?"

"Last week," Martin said. "Bink and some guys cornered me in the locker room. Said I was hurting the team if I didn't. Matt, will they kick me out of school if they find out? What am I going to do?"

Just then, the list was handed down the row to Matt. Coach Charles was standing at the end of the row, a scowl on his face. The players sitting in front of Matt turned and stared at him as he held the document.

Dear God, he prayed. What should I do?

What would you do?

If Matt supports the board's decision, turn to page 50.
If he decides to oppose it, turn to page 55.

"Oh well," Matt said with a wink, "the Bible says 'an eye for an eye and a tooth for a tooth'. too! So far, I've kept all my teeth!"

Dee Dee looked at him strangely.

"Anyway," Matt said, uncomfortable under Dee Dee's gaze, "what you do on the field is something completely different. You can count on me. I'll always do my best for you guys out there."

"Yeah, rook," Dee Dee said and walked away.

Matt's aggressive hitting caught Coach Charles' eye, and soon he was playing more. He liked everyone's praise and played full-tilt on every down. Opposing players didn't appreciate Matt's style, and plays often ended in shouting and shoving matches. Matt was never penalized and continued his hard-nosed tackling.

During the next-to-last game of the season against the Buna Bumblebees, one of the Bees' tight ends delivered a block to Matt's blind side that sent him tumbling. Though the block was clean, Matt came up swinging. He caught the Bee player flush in the stomach with a wicked left hook. The tight end went down on one knee, clutching his stomach.

The referee threw his yellow flag, penalized the Eagles 15 yards and tossed Matt out of the game. Matt's backup was a nervous freshman, and the Buna quarterback capitalized on the young guy's inexperience—which led to a Bumblebee victory.

The following week, the Echo of the Eagle Empire, the school newspaper, ran an unsigned humor column on the game. In it, Matt became Samson and the Buna players became donkeys—which Matt slew with his own jawbone. The article also made references to Matt's roles as head of the First Church youth group and the school's Christian athletes' fellowship—which he co-founded. It compared those activities unfavorably to Matt's now-infamous fighting style.

Matt was enraged by the article and demanded a retraction. But the editor was unmoved. "If the shoe fits, wear it, Matt," she said firmly.

Stung, Matt reread the article. Could the criticism be valid? he wondered.

What would you do?

If Matt stews about the criticism, turn to page 64.
If he takes the point of the article seriously, turn to page 74.

In time, youth group trips and time with Gaile or Martin grew more important to Matt, and his single-minded devotion to fitness fell by the wayside. Without football, Matt found a world of things to do in the fall. He'd never had so much time on his hands. It scared him—just a little.

One Sunday night, he and Gaile went to hear Vinnie "The Studebaker" Cleagle, a star basketball player for the Houston Rockets, speak at First Church. Vinnie was from East Texas and often returned to speak in his old stomping grounds.

"Man, you better know The Studebaker was flyin' high when he was drafted by the Warriors in the first round," Vinnie said with an infectious laugh. "I was gonna turn the NBA on its ear, man. Look out, Lakers, 'cause The Studebaker's comin' through!

"Didn't work out that way, though. Guys who grew up in the inner city just laughed when I showed them my moves. I sat on the bench all that year and most of the next year too. Wasn't hardly even gettin' trash minutes. Finally, the Warriors let me go. Waived me outright. People, let me tell you I was *low.*"

Matt was bored with Vinnie's story. He knew how it ended. Vinnie rededicated his life to basketball, caught on with the Rockets and became a big star. Same old line. But The Studebaker surprised him.

"You know how I got back?" he asked the audience. "Jesus. Jesus did it. But first, he had to break me. Break me of my pride. Break me of my complacency. Break me of my bad habits. I had to get so low I had nowhere else to go.

"The Lord waited until I admitted I was playing basketball for all the wrong reasons. He waited until I admitted success and money had become gods to me. He waited until I admitted that, without him, I was nothing. And after I admitted all that, Jesus took me back."

After The Studebaker's talk, Gaile and Matt walked the quiet streets.

"You've been quiet, Matt," Gaile said. "Still thinking about what Vinnie said?"

"Uh huh, I guess so," Matt said. "What he said makes sense. But it all sounded too slick, too pat. Like he's given that same speech a hundred times before."

"That doesn't make it any less true," she said.

"Oh, I know. It just seems so ... so Hollywood. He makes it

all sound so cut-and-dried. Give your life to Jesus, and he gives you what you want. For Vinnie it was basketball. For me it's football. For you it might be a marching band scholarship to Baylor. I just have trouble with that kind of thinking."

"I'm not sure he was saying that," Gaile said. "I'm not even sure he'd want to put himself up as a role model. But I do know this: Since you left football, you've been searching for something. I don't know what it is, but you seem ... I dunno ... restless or something. Does that sound too dramatic?"

"Naw, not really. Gaile, I'm confused about what to do. Should I do like Vinnie did and rededicate myself to football? Or should I stay out of it because I tend to make it too important?"

What would you do?

If Matt follows The Studebaker's model, turn to page 58.
If he doesn't follow Vinnie's suggestion, turn to page 101.

"You win, James," Matt said with a cheerfulness he didn't feel. "I couldn't chug that much beer. I've never done it, actually. It probably wouldn't stay down. I'd be huggin' the stone pony all night. I must decline your generous offer." He bowed elegantly to the girls, who giggled.

James was livid. "And I say you're scared, rook," James shouted. "You've never had a drink in your life, have you— mamma's boy? I'll bet you never even had a girl. Never thrown a pass, never had a drink, never had a girl. You're not an Eagle; you're a chicken! Do you hear me, you're yellow! And you're too yellow to do anything when someone calls you a chicken."

"You're drunk, James ol' boy," Matt responded. "And I don't fight Eagles. I thought we were a team."

James lurched forward to swing at Matt but was caught by Dee Dee and Bink. "Hey, no fightin'. That's Dad's one rule," Dee Dee said. "Bink, drag Mr. Macho here to the tub and sober him up with some ice and cold water. If Coach Charles shows up and finds him like this, James is gone for the season."

Dee Dee turned to the crowd. "Show's over folks." He winked covertly at Matt. "Good job, rook."

Matt walked out on the porch, where Martin was sitting on a window sill. He'd seen the whole thing.

"I think something important happened here," Martin said, forgetting his anger at Matt for going into the party.

"What? I've made an enemy for life," Matt moaned. "I've alienated the entire team. I looked like a coward."

"Naw, more important than any of that. Besides, James won't remember any of this in the morning. The point is you took a stand. Dee Dee respects you. Some of the other guys do too. I can tell.

"Matt," Martin lowered his voice even more, "we need to stand up for our beliefs on this team."

Matt whirled and stared at Martin. "Say what!?" But Martin was deadly serious.

"No foolin'. That talk James and Dee Dee gave about last year's Eagles was all true. They didn't have any team spirit, no chemistry, no nothing. But their remedy is all wrong. Having more parties won't do it. Taking a stand for the Lord might."

"Marty, we're nobodies. They'll laugh us off the bus. Can you imagine me talking to James about my faith?"

Martin thought for a minute. "Yes."

"Now look here. I'm not ashamed of my faith or anything. But maybe it'd be better just to lead by example, you know? Sometimes it's okay to talk about God, but you've gotta see there's a time and a place for everything," Matt said urgently.

"That's exactly what I'm sayin' now, Matt."

What would you do?

If Matt agrees with Martin to share their faith with the whole team, turn to page 66.

If Matt decides to keep it quiet and just lead by example, turn to page 78.

On the last leg of Saturday's meet, Matt put on a strong kick and surged past the pace-setters into the lead. As he turned the final corner, he heard the members of First Church's youth group cheering in the stands. That gave him enough of an adrenaline rush to fight off a late kick by a runner from Kirbyville and break the tape.

The cross country team, the youth group, even Gaile poured onto the track and pounded Matt on the back. He was on top of the world. This is what it's all about, Matt thought to himself. Prestige. These guys think I'm somebody! His teammates carried him on their shoulders to the field house.

The euphoria continued throughout the next week. Even some of the football players congratulated him in the hallways.

■

The next several weeks were an emotional roller coaster for Matt. When he'd win, he'd be disappointed if he didn't set the meet record. When he'd lose, he'd brood for days and train an extra hour each night.

In time, Matt spent less and less time involved in church activities. Gaile tried to take up jogging to be with him, but she simply couldn't keep up. Eventually she quit trying as well. She couldn't compete with cross country in his life.

Finally, on the bus to the district meet, Coach Dallas took Matt aside.

"Son, lemme tell you something straight here. You listenin'?"

"Uh, yeah, Coach. Sure thing. What's up?"

"Matt, I never thought I'd say this to an athlete, but you're takin' this stuff way too seriously. You've become an obsessive. The other runners tell me you've dropped out of just about everything. And I hear the other teachers say your grades this semester aren't all that hot either."

Matt stared at his running shoes. "Aw, Coach, it isn't as bad as all that. It's just that I've finally found something I'm good at. Before cross country, I was a nobody. This is the first time in my life people notice me in the halls."

"Listen son, you've wrapped your whole self-worth, your whole identity, into this cross country thing," Dallas said. "And if you keep it up, you're in for a big fall."

Matt was stunned at Dallas' words. Am I really like that? he thought frantically. But as the bus neared Hardin-Bush High School, Matt's thoughts returned to the meet.

This late in the season, the weather had turned blustery and chilly. A light drizzle fell off and on throughout the afternoon. Hardin-Bush's cross country course wound in lazy circles around the campus.

But Matt was oblivious to the cold and rain. When the starter's gun sounded, he was off in a blur of motion. Nobody was going to set the pace for him today!

The cross country route skirted a section of forest bulldozed by a lumber company. The terrain looked like a lunar landscape. "What a waste," Matt idly thought as he continued to lead the pack by a healthy margin.

Crack!

The sound was impossibly loud in his ears. A millisecond later, a bolt of pain screamed up from his ankle and hit his brain with an electric shock. Matt fell like a broken doll, his ankle twisted in a grotesque position.

"Oh dear God, not my ankle. Not now! Please, dear God, don't let this happen to me. Please!" he screamed, not caring if anyone heard him.

After several other runners passed, a runner from Hardin-Bush ran up and crouched by his side.

"Stay still, don't move, you'll just hurt yourself worse. It'll be okay, I promise. I'll get help. Just don't move."

Just by looking at his ankle, Matt could tell it was broken. He found himself weighing his options through the fog of pain.

This year's over, kaput, finished, he thought. Depending on how bad the break is, next year could be out of the question too.

Matt could hear voices shouting in the distance. Sounds like Coach Dallas, he mused. At least he's not the type to say, "I told you so."

Question is: What do I do now? I'm back to being a zero again. A nobody again. Worse, I'm a nobody on one leg.

What would you do?

If Matt makes the best of his situation, turn to page 72.
If he's glum and moody over his bad break, turn to page 84.

Karen O'Hara—better known as Ol' Lady O'Hara—was also the swimming coach, by virtue of having competed as a freshman in college. She wasn't one of Matt's favorite teachers.

After a couple of "swim-offs" against members of last year's team, Coach O'Hara let Matt on the team. Some team members had been swimming seriously since they were small children. Matt was strong enough to compete, but not yet skilled enough to win.

Swim meets came and went. Long bus rides, moldy dressing rooms, cold pools and last-place finishes. In fact, Matt finished dead last at most meets—though he occasionally beat some of the younger swimmers. O'Hara also made the team study on the bus, so there was little of the horseplay and hijinks he'd enjoyed with the JV football team. He got better each week, but he'd still finish behind the more polished swimmers.

Matt's frustration came to a head in practice the week before a big meet with Hardin-Bush. The team members were swimming endurance-building laps, and Matt was lagging behind even the younger swimmers. His heart obviously wasn't in it.

Suddenly, his daydreams were shattered by Coach O'Hara shouting at the top of her lungs. "Matt, get out of the water. Now! If you're not going to try, then don't waste my time. So get out now! Do you hear me? Now!"

Confused, Matt kept swimming. "Aw, Coach O'Hara, I am trying, I'm just worn out. I'll keep up."

"No you won't, mister," she screamed. "I've had enough of your half-hearted attitude. You're not even trying. How do you think that makes me feel after I stuck my neck out for you?"

Matt stopped swimming and treaded water. "Look, Coach O'Hara. I'm the one who keeps finishing last in meets, not you. I make every practice. I make every meet. I'm the one taking a beating out here. What do you want from me?"

"What do I want? The question is: What do you want, Matt? Are you going to stick with swimming—and give it your best shot? Or are you going to give up because you've finished last a couple of times? What'll it be, Matt?" she demanded.

What would you do?

If Matt sticks with swimming, turn to page 14.
If he gets discouraged and leaves, turn to page 22.

"Okay, I guess you're right," Martin conceded. "Maybe it'll be fun."

"Good man, Marty." Matt grinned and slapped Martin on the shoulder.

■

Matt and Martin arrived after 8:30, and the party was already in full swing. All the lights were on in Dee Dee's house, and the guys could feel the bass booming from Dee Dee's giant stereo. As they walked across the yard, they could just make out the forms of two couples making out under the willow tree.

The door was standing open. Just before they walked in, Martin put his hand on Matt's arm.

"Uh ... confession time. I've never been to a party like this before."

"Aw, it's just like a church party," Matt said with a nervous laugh. "Actually, I've never been to a party like this either." He took a deep breath.

"Well, I guess you gotta start somewhere."

Just then, one of the seniors dashed out the front door and heaved himself into the bushes, retching violently.

"Yeah, but is this *really* the place to start?" Martin asked.

"Man, don't back out on me now!" Matt responded. "If we don't go, we're not part of the team. They'll think we're a couple of 'holy Joes.' "

Martin didn't say anything but had a quizzical look on his face.

"Well, stay out here," Matt barked. "Be a party-pooper for all I care. I'm going in!"

Matt stormed in the front door. The living room was draped with banners: "All the Way to State!" "Welcome New Eagles!" "We're #1!" Under the signs, couples were dancing to the thundering beat. It didn't take him long to notice that most of the cheerleaders, many of the drill team members and virtually all of the best-looking girls from the band were there.

"Yo! Rook! Front and center!" It was Dee Dee, with a beautiful freshman girl with long, long brown hair and a short, short skirt sitting in his lap. "Welcome to my humble abode. Your first duty, rookie, is to get me and Julie here another brewski. Then help yourself to one. They're in the bathroom. In the tub."

Matt smiled lamely. He'd seen what alcohol had done even in his own family, how it had ruined lives. He knew what the Bible said about drinking to excess. He'd always tried to remain true to his faith. And he'd always avoided getting caught in situations like this one. Now all of the false confidence he'd displayed in front of Martin vanished.

"Give me strength," he prayed.

"Yeah, sure, Dee Dee," he mumbled.

But Dee Dee had already turned his full attention back to the thin freshman with the doe-like eyes. Good, Matt thought, I'll just disappear. He's already forgotten about me.

Suddenly, Genie Salat, Wanda Bolin, Therese Morales and Soozi Charles—the coach's daughter—surrounded Matt in the hall.

"Look girls, here's our new backup quarterback," Genie said as she pressed in front of him.

"Ooh, you're cute," Wanda teased, running the back of her hand along his cheek.

"I'm glad you made the team," Therese said huskily. "I'll bet you look great in uniform."

"Honestly, Therese," Soozi said with mock impatience. "You think they *all* look great in uniform. But let's not frighten this one off," she blushed.

Matt could smell the liquor on the breath of all the girls— particularly Therese and Soozi, the two seniors. Genie and Wanda were in his class, but they'd had little contact with him over the years. Genie and James had been together nearly two years. None of the girls had paid much attention to Matt in the past.

"Well, aren't you going to say anything?" Wanda cooed. "Or are you the strong, silent type?"

What would you do?

If Matt laps up the sudden attention, turn to page 41.
If he keeps the attention in perspective, turn to page 53.

Matt stood quietly for a moment. "Maybe God just doesn't want me in organized sports. You know, I kinda like having afternoons off for the first time since I started Peewee Football. And we get more time together, don't we?"

Gaile was confused by Matt's sudden shift in mood. "Yes, but ..."

"No buts. My mind's made up, Gaile. As of now, I'm out of sports. I don't need the hassle or the pain. I sure don't need taking abuse from Coach Charles or any other coach."

Matt eventually drew away from organized sports completely. He even quit attending the games, preferring to stay home and watch television or take Gaile to a movie.

The weeks stretched into months, and Matt's resolve became more entrenched. Eventually Matt took pride in *not* being involved in sports.

One day during lunch break, Matt stood with several guys outside the cafeteria, telling "dumb jock" stories about his days playing football.

"Those dudes are animals, lemme tell you," Matt said. "I kid you not, that guy has a serious personal relationship with the tackling dummy. Thank goodness he wears a helmet on the practice field or we'd never tell them apart! I mean, all those football guys are dorks!"

Matt was too busy laughing at his own stories to notice that the other guys were motioning him to knock it off. The laughter stopped, and Matt felt a presence behind him.

He peeked over his shoulder and saw the imposing figure of Vernon Thomas, the starting weakside linebacker. Vernon was cracking his knuckles and scowling. When Matt turned back around, the knot of guys who'd been listening to him had vanished.

Blind choice:

Without looking ahead, turn to page 116 or page 21 to continue the story.

Matt's answer came following the next track meet. It was a tough meet with several larger schools. Matt ran his best cross country time ever and still finished last, more than a minute behind the next finisher.

Coach Dallas ambled up. "Sorry about that son," he said. "You did your best, and that's all that's important to me. Disappointed?"

Matt thought a moment. "No, I guess not. In fact, I feel pretty good. I knew with a mile to go I wasn't going to catch the rest of the pack, but I enjoyed the run."

"Well, that's a change," Coach Dallas said, chuckling.

"I've been praying about it, Coach," Matt explained. "If I win, I want to give God the glory. If I lose and do my best—he's still just as pleased. Right?"

Coach Dallas nodded. "Matt, with that kind of attitude, you'll always be a winner. I promise you that."

As the cross country season progressed, Matt continued to run hard in every race. He placed high in some meets, low in others. When the season ended, Matt continued to run for the pleasure of it through the woods around the school. He'd find a rhythm and would suddenly realize that he'd been unconsciously praying or thinking about God as he ran.

Then came football tryouts. By the time two-a-days started in August, every ounce of fat was burned from Matt's body. He tackled two-a-days with the same attitude he'd approached cross country. Win or lose, he gave his best.

The two weeks were up faster than he ever dreamed possible, and it was time for Coach Charles once again to post the varsity roster.

Blind choice:

Without looking ahead, turn to page 24 or page 43 to see if Matt makes the team.

Matt and Martin inconspicuously edged out of the crowd toward Martin's car. They decided they wanted no part of the party. Neither felt like God would want them to go. They hoped to slip away unnoticed.

But just as they were getting in Martin's car, Dee Dee and a group of seniors passed by, heading for their cars. Dee Dee called out to Matt and Martin.

"Yo! Rooks! You boys bring the chips tonight. Right?"

Matt and Martin looked at each other in panic.

"Sorry, Dee Dee! Martin and I can't make the bash tonight."

"Yeah!" Martin said brightly. "Something's come up. I bet it'll be the best party of the year too."

Dee Dee stopped by his new cherry-red Toyota.

"So, what's the deal, rooks? I thought we were going to be a team this year," Dee Dee said coldly. "Why aren't you coming?"

Dee Dee looked at James and said in a stage whisper. "This better be good."

What would you do?

If Matt tells them about his faith, turn to page 112.
If Matt makes up an excuse for not going, turn to page 8.

Matt pushed his way through the guys gathered around the roster posted outside the old field house. Under quarterback, there were two names, his and Ky Sams'. Ky's name was listed first.

Matt whirled and said through clenched teeth, "I'm not being the second-stringer for anyone, ever again!" He walked away and never set foot on the football stadium grounds again.

When the team did well under Ky, Matt's mood continued to blacken. At first he blamed himself for not working out with the team. Then he blamed Coach Charles for never really giving him a chance. Though he never admitted it to himself, he eventually blamed God.

The Eagles had a strong team Matt's senior year. Martin made the team, and his Christian influence helped several players make a stand for Christ. They grew together as a team and had as much fun during practices or on the long bus rides as they did playing together.

The Eagles won all the way to regionals before falling to a bigger, faster team from La Vega.

Matt stayed home and thought about the "might bes" and "should've beens" and "could bes"—blaming everyone else but himself.

And that night, he established a lifestyle of blaming others that took him to the end of his days.

The End

"Uh ... look Genie. You've got to be the sexiest, best-lookin' girl I've ever met. No foolin'. There's not a guy out there who wouldn't give his left arm to be with you."

Genie blushed. "Flatterer. You're not so hard to take yourself, Matt." She leaned even closer until his whole world was those eyes, those lips, that hair and, oh, that perfume. Matt felt dizzy.

"But, I gotta tell you this. I'm seein' someone else," he said quickly, before he changed his mind. "You probably don't know her. Her name is Gaile. She's a sophomore. She's not head cheer-leader or anything, but she's special to me. And even if she wasn't, you'd think less of me if I dumped her for you. I'm not that kinda guy."

Genie jerked her hand from Matt's arm.

"I can't believe you, Matt Brand! What made you think I was interested in you? You must have some kind of ego, buster! I don't need a second-team quarterback hitting on me!"

She fled from the room, but Matt could see she was crying. Nice job, he thought to himself. Smooth move. You're a regular lady-killer, son.

Bink, Dee Dee and some of the others strolled into the bath-room.

"Hey, what's eatin' her?"

"What'd you say, rookie?"

"Gentlemen," Dee Dee said grandly, "I think Miss Salat is suffering from a broken heart. And this unlikely specimen is the culprit."

"What? You dumped Genie Salat?" a sophomore gasped. "She's like only the foxiest babe in the school! I can't believe it. No way! Hey, he's not gay or something, is he?"

Bink shook his head in mock sympathy. "Mr. Brand here is an honorable man. He's dating that little what's-her-name sopho-more. Can't say I blame him. Genie's way out of his league."

The guys turned to leave. Bink turned back at the door.

"Rookie, you're one stupid dude. Know that? You'll never live this down."

■

Bink was right. The other team members, save Martin—and James, for obvious reasons—razzed Matt all week. He took few snaps in practice, Coach Charles preferring to get Dee Dee ready for the game with Center. Matt spent most of the week on the sidelines.

"I'll say this," Bink said as he passed, walking toward the water fountain. "That little church girl of yours must be incredible in Bible school."

"Yeah, I hear she gives great communion," another said. All the players roared in laughter.

■

The game against the Center Panthers was a defensive struggle. Neither team could sustain long drives. Matt stood on the sidelines, his uniform unmarked by grass stains, mud or blood.

At the start of the third quarter, Dee Dee changed a straight running play into an option around right end. At the snap, he faked to the fullback, then darted down the line. The safety wasn't fooled. He hit Dee Dee in the hip. The quarterback went down with a grunt.

Coach Charles cursed, then looked down the sideline.

"Brand! Get in there, boy! What're you waiting for?"

Matt's mind raced as he headed for the field. This is my chance, he thought. This could be my door to a starting quarterback position. But—Matt's heart skipped a beat—what if I fail?

Blind choice:

Without looking ahead, turn to page 34 or page 37 to continue the story.

Matt's decision came after several nights of prayer. "Football, Dad. I gotta play football." He stood in the kitchen doorway watching his dad wash the dishes.

Matt's father put down the sponge. "I'm glad, son," he said. "I enjoyed it a lot. You know I got into my college on a partial football scholarship. I never could've gone to college otherwise. I knew I never would be fast or big or strong enough to play in the NFL, but football taught me a lot."

Matt furrowed his brow. "Dad, be honest. If I play up to my fullest potential—if I give it my dead-level best shot—will I be good enough to get a football scholarship?"

Matt's dad mused a moment. "Well, son, I guess we'll never know if you don't try, will we?"

Under his dad's guidance, Matt began a training program that continued through the winter and spring. Nearly every day, Gaile swam laps with him at the YMCA, Martin ran with him through the woods, and his father coached him on the nuances of football.

By the start of summer two-a-days, Matt's frail physique had matured into a solid, 190 pounds of muscle. He was the first one on the playing field at 6 a.m. on the first day of two-a-days. As he loosened up, Coach Charles drove up and watched him from under the stands.

Could this be Matt's big break, or will he face disappointment again?

Blind choice:

Without looking ahead, turn to page 24 or page 43 to see if Matt makes the team.

All the euphoria and confidence from the previous weeks vanished as he reflected on the night's game. He'd lost, lost, lost. He couldn't get it out of his mind.

Matt talked to no one on the bus ride home. His dad was at the newspaper pasting up tomorrow's edition, so the house was dark and lonely. Matt sat in his father's chair with the lights out and brooded.

I lost the game, he thought. Singlehanded. My life is in ashes and I don't have anyone to blame but myself. Let's face it Mattie-boy: You choked. You blew it for yourself and everyone else. Wherever I go from now on, people will talk as I pass, and they'll say, "Yeah, that's the dufus who let the whole team down. Ruined the best season in our history." I don't blame them either. I wish I could just disappear. No one will even miss me.

There was a knock on the door. Matt ignored it at first, then walked to the door. "Probably James or Bink here to chew me out one last time."

When he opened the door, his heart skipped a beat.

"Surprise! Surprise!"

On his porch, spilling across the yard and out to the street was a crowd of people, all shouting and singing. A number of cars had their headlights pointed at the front door as well. On the porch were Matt's girlfriend Gaile, Martin, youth minister Robyn McGregor and most of the youth group. Many football players were there too, including Dee Dee. Standing by the mailbox was his father, who shrugged. He pointed at Robyn, who'd organized the whole thing.

"Oh, Matt we're so proud of you!" Gaile said as she gave him a hug. "You were wonderful."

As the people filed in the house, loaded down with soft drinks and snacks, Matt sputtered, "But ... but I lost the championship game."

Dee Dee grabbed Matt's head in a hammerlock and shouted in his ear. "Rook, how dumb can you get? If you hadn't played like gangbusters all season, we wouldn't have got to the championship game in the first place!"

Dee Dee let Matt stand up and put his hands on his shoulders.

"C'mon rookie, winning isn't everything. Even I know that."

As the two quarterbacks walked into Matt's house, Robyn

stood to one side crying tears of joy. Matt's father walked up and put his hand on her shoulder. He was crying as well.

"Must be the dust," he murmured.

"No," she responded, sniffling. "I think it's love."

The End

Coach Terry Dallas was tall and handsome, and the only coach with any professional football experience. He coached the 7th- and 8th-grade football teams, the varsity cross country team and, in his spare time, worked out with the varsity defensive backs. He stood at the field house with the cross country team lined up in front of him.

"Well, well, well. It's good to see you back to do a little running this year. I had most of you last year. But in case you don't know him, boys, I want you to meet newcomer Matt Brand."

Matt ducked his head and scuffed his feet. Everybody knew everybody in the school. But Matt knew Dallas was just picking on him.

"Gentlemen, as you may know, I've got a different philosophy than most coaches," Dallas continued. "If you show up every day and work out, as far as I'm concerned, you're on the team. We'll have a full-scale run on Wednesdays. The top six finishers, plus one alternate, will compete in that week's meet. So each week you've got as much chance as anyone else."

Matt liked the sound of Dallas' system. Plenty of incentives and—even if you didn't do well one week—you stayed in shape, hoping to make it the following week.

"Now here's the surprise," Dallas said. "The cross country season doesn't really start for several weeks. But I've arranged a practice meet with Warren and Chester tomorrow. So we're going to have our little competition today instead of Wednesday. Let's stretch 'em out, boys."

Matt looked at the coach in disbelief. "Now? You mean right now?"

Dallas caught Matt's eye. "Now," he said.

Dallas ran with the team, setting an easy pace. The route wound through the pine forest around the school. Matt had to work hard to keep up most of the way. But the two-a-day workouts of the previous two weeks paid dividends. Matt finished sixth.

Back at the field house, Dallas clapped Matt on the shoulder.

"Not bad, son—especially since you've never trained in cross country. I'm glad you're here. You'll be a good example for the younger runners."

Matt felt the warmth of Dallas' acceptance—unlike Charles' icy disdain. It was nice to be wanted.

"Uh ... Coach? One question," Matt said as they walked to the showers. "Wednesdays after practice are when we have the determining race for Saturday's meets, right?"

"Right. And?"

"That's when I have youth group meetings at my church. I don't know if you know, Coach," Matt was talking fast now, "but I'm the youth group president. Is there some way I could, like, run against time on Tuesday or Thursday to see if I get to run on Saturday?"

Dallas didn't say anything as he continued to mop his neck with a towel.

Matt added. "Or, uh, I don't suppose you'd consider changing the tryout day, would you?" Dallas arched his eyebrows. "I didn't think so," Matt mumbled.

"Sorry, Matt, I'd love to have you on the team," Dallas said. "More than you know. But you know I can't make exceptions. It wouldn't be fair to the other guys. I'm afraid you're going to have to choose between the youth group and the cross country team."

What would you do?

If Matt decides to stay on the team, turn to page 51.
If Matt decides to stay with the youth group, turn to page 60.

"I'll be honest with you, Dee Dee. I just don't think it's right—not for me, anyway," Matt said, at peace with himself. "I'm sure not judging anybody. Lord knows I do enough things on my own. But I just don't feel I can go."

"Me neither," Martin said.

"Oh, this is just great," James drawled. "A couple of 'holy rollers' on the team. Too good to drink with the guys."

"James, Dee Dee—you've seen me play. Martin too. We'll give you 100 percent. We always have. We'll be there when the team needs us. I just don't think drinking together is what'll make this team special."

"I'm not talking about drinking, you stupid rookie," James shouted. "I'm talking about getting together, forming a team, working together, playing together. Nobody has to get drunk at the parties. Do they, Bink?"

"Naw, it's cool, it's cool. Guys do whatever they want." Some of the other seniors punched Bink playfully in the back.

"Yeah, whatever they want," they snickered.

"I believe you, James," Matt said. "You're a straight shooter. I respect your beliefs. Please try to understand mine. This is a personal decision that doesn't reflect on anyone else. I just don't believe God wants me somewhere where there's that much drinking."

"Your loss, rook," Dee Dee said. He jumped in his car and careened off, followed by the other players.

"Well, that went over like a lead balloon," Matt sighed.

"Maybe we oughta talk to Robyn," Martin offered. "She might have some good advice."

"Okay. Couldn't hurt."

Robyn McGregor, the youth minister at First Church, was sympathetic. "Gosh, guys, there's no easy way to share your faith. Taking a stand—especially an unpopular one like you two just did—usually means you'll catch some grief. But believe it or not, it usually helps someone else who's wavering—someone you may not even know about."

"I guess that's true," Matt said with a sigh. "I just don't see anybody who's even close to 'wavering.' "

"Also, you two are laying the groundwork for next year,"

Robyn said. "When you're seniors, *you'll* set the tone. You'll see. It'll become cool to be a Christian when the leaders are Christians. But you have to start now."

"The way I figure it," Martin said, "we can either make a statement about this—right up front—and hope some of the other guys join us. Or we can just try to lead by example. You know, not make a big deal about it, but quietly be good witnesses."

"Well, that's a decision you guys need to make," Robyn said.

What would you do?

If Matt and Martin decide to be vocal witnesses, turn to page 66.
If Matt decides to lead by example, turn to page 78.

▼

But after a couple of days, Matt had convinced himself that The Studebaker was only in it for the money. As the days wore on, Matt found more and more things to dislike about the guys who played sports—any sport. He hated how they endlessly re-hashed the previous Friday night's game. He despised how the coaches wasted precious class time talking about football instead of civics or history or government or health.

Matt went from ignoring school athletes to being antagonistic toward them. He never missed a chance to say something cutting when an athlete spoke in class. He ridiculed all the "dumb jocks" behind their backs whenever he could.

One day Matt was telling stories about the athletes to a group of guys outside the cafeteria. He laughingly referred to them as the "dorks with the brains of tackling dummies." But then all the guys he was talking to began to walk away. They could see Vernon Thomas, the weakside linebacker, coming up behind Matt. He'd heard it all.

Matt turned around, and gulped.

Blind choice:

Without looking ahead, turn to page 116 or page 21 to continue the story.

▼

After a few more minutes on the bench, Matt walked into the press room where reporters were interviewing the winning coach and players. Several reporters rushed over to Matt.

"Your thoughts, Matt," one local TV reporter said.

"Well, it was a good season. No one expected this much out of us. But with the Lord's help we stayed healthy, and we gave the La Vega guys a run for their money. They simply had the better team."

"Matt, you seem to be handling this pretty well," the reporter continued.

Here it comes, Matt thought. My chance to say something publicly about what I believe, and my knees are knocking, and my mouth's gone dry! I never realized this could be so scary!

"Before the game I … I asked Jesus to help me accept the outcome—whatever it turned out to be. I'm thankful he gives me the strength to play. I just want to do my best for him."

As Matt walked off, the reporter turned to the camera operator and subtly signaled to keep the tape running.

"That was Matt Brand, the Eagles junior quarterback, who lost tonight to the powerful La Vega Pirates. But no matter what the final score in this contest Matt Brand emerged a winner. This is Carroll Johns reporting for Channel 7 News. "

■

Several guys from the team and from school commented to Matt about his interview. A few team members talked to him more about his faith. It was good for Matt and great for team members whose hearts were changed.

Matt's heart swelled every chance he got to honor God with his athletics. He played out his senior year in football, taking the team all the way to state. He then went on to play for Lamar University, each year improving his game and taking the team farther than the previous year.

After college, he went on staff with Athletes in Action—an organization dedicated to using sports to reach others for Christ. He toured several nations sharing his faith with athletes from all parts of the globe. But each time he shared, he always thought back to that first time in high school, when the reporter gave him the chance to tell about Jesus—and he did.

The End

Vernon wasn't pleased.

"Dorks, huh, punk?" he asked with a snarl. He shoved Matt. "Dumb jocks, are we?" He shoved Matt down. Stung, Matt came up swinging. Vernon, a veteran of dozens of brawls on the football field, blocked Matt's right and leveled him with a single punch to the jaw.

Blinded by the pain and tears, Matt struggled to his feet. Vernon sneered at him. "Tackling dummy, little man?" Vernon placed his cowboy boot on Matt's chest and pushed him back down.

■

Word of Matt's humiliation spread around the school. When Martin tried to talk to him after class, Matt complained about athletes even more. Vernon's punch only confirmed Matt's disgust.

That night at the youth group, Matt sat in a corner, nursing his sore jaw—and wounded pride—while Robyn talked about labels and stereotypes.

"The Bible is full of labels," she said. "You know the story of the Good Samaritan? The Jews hated the Samaritans, and vice versa. So it was a big deal the time Jesus drank with the Samaritan woman at the well. What does that say about Jesus' attitude?"

"I guess that Jesus hated barriers," Gaile said. "Labels too. He accepted people without putting them in a box."

"Bingo!" Robyn exclaimed. "He hated stereotypes. The Samaritan woman couldn't believe a Jew was actually in Samaria, much less that he was talking to her. And Jesus still hates the labels we put on people. It doesn't take much imagination to guess how he feels about people using racial slurs, does it?"

"Nope," Martin said. "He hates any kind of stereotype."

"Right!" Robyn said. "That's because stereotypes make it easy to judge people and make yourself look good. So-and-so is a prep, and preps are jerks. So since I'm not a prep, I must be okay. See how that's a cop-out?"

Matt focused on what Robyn was saying. He didn't like it.

"Robyn," Gaile asked, "does that mean every time someone stereotypes another person that it hurts Jesus?"

"That's right, Gaile," Robyn said. "It hurts him very much."

After a few seconds, Matt spoke so softly Robyn could barely hear him.

" 'Dumb jock' is one of those words too, isn't it Robyn?"

"Yes, yes, I suppose so, Matt, if it's used intentionally to hurt someone. Why?"

Martin and Gaile looked at Matt as he stared at his hands. "No reason," he said, but conflicting thoughts reeled inside his head.

At the break, Gaile stayed in the circle with Matt after everyone left.

"That stuff you said about labeling people made a lot of sense," Matt said. "Maybe I never gave any of the athletes a chance. I can't really say that I know anybody on the varsity. But I really don't know how I could now."

"That's a good point," Gaile said. "It looks to me that there are two ways to get to know them. You can just try to be more attentive and approachable out of class. Or you can get back involved in sports. Either way will probably work."

"Yeah, sounds like it could work." But which way should I go? he wondered.

What would you do?

If Matt decides to get to know more athletes, turn to page 70.
If Matt decides to get involved in sports, turn to page 85.

"Good question, Dee Dee," Matt said after a whispered prayer. "I play as hard as I can on every play. I believe we ought to do everything for God's glory. But I never want to hurt anybody.

"I know Bink and James get all worked up for the games by imagining that the other guys are their enemies. Me, I get all worked up knowing they're just guys out to do their best too. They're like friends I haven't met—not enemies. Whoops! Guess I was preaching to you, Dee Dee. Sorry."

"I don't mind," Dee Dee said. "Seems you get the same results as Bink. You just don't hurt anybody in the process. So what about this 'turn the other cheek' business?"

"Well, when I get a late hit that ought to be a flagrant foul, I just stand there and don't hit back. About half the time the ref only sees your retaliation anyway, and *you* get tossed out of the game. Ever notice that? I just turn and walk away. Besides, that makes 'em *really* mad."

"Matt, you're kinda corny, but you're all right, you know? I'll tell you one thing: I sure like your attitude better than Coach Charles' 'win at any cost' approach."

"Yeah, well the way I figure it, this is only a game. I think it's Galatians 4:18 that says something like 'It's fine to be zealous, provided the purpose is good ...' And football's a 'good thing,' but who's gonna remember the score of a single game 10 years from now? It's just not that important in the big scheme of things. How you treat people, how you affect them—that stuff sticks around."

"I guess that makes sense," Dee Dee said. "Maybe we'll talk about this again sometime."

The next week against the Center Panthers, Dee Dee went down with a hip pointer at the start of the second half. As he was being carried to the bench, he looked up at Matt as he passed.

"Hey rookie!" Dee Dee said, his face distorted by pain. "Do this thing 'zealously' for me tonight, okay?"

"Okay, Dee Dee," Matt said.

Zealously it is! And he ran out onto the field. But then a horrid thought raced through his mind: What if I blow it?

Blind choice:

Without looking ahead, turn to page 34 or page 37 to continue the story.

After a sleepless night, Matt met Genie before class. She ran up and hugged him before he could speak.

"Matt, honey, I was so hurt you didn't call last night," Genie said with a hint of mischief in her eyes. "I figured I must be losing my appeal, so I'm going by the boutique after school and buy something special just for you. I'll be happy to model it for you tonight. Just the two of us." Her lip quivered in apprehension.

"Uh, yeah, Genie. Sure. I'll be there."

Still, Matt felt uncomfortable with the physical nature of their relationship. Genie always had a couple of drinks, then would get aggressive as they made out. A couple of times Matt had to catch himself before they went too far. His stance only made Genie more aggressive when they were alone together.

In time, he grew concerned about her drinking as well. It seemed they couldn't do anything without a couple of drinks first.

Still, Matt and Genie stayed together. She'd never had a guy who treated her with such respect. Or restraint. He'd never been with a girl who made every head turn when she walked into a room. And it just seemed natural for a quarterback—even the backup—and a cheerleader to be together.

■

The night of the big game against the Center Panthers started like other games that season. From his position on the sidelines, Matt could see the trick-or-treaters in the neighborhood surrounding the stadium. It was Halloween, and he'd forgotten all about it.

At halftime, Coach Charles switched offenses. The Panther defense was too tough for the Eagles' pro style offense.

As the second half opened, Dee Dee called an option around right end. But the safety didn't fall for Dee Dee's fakes and nailed him on the hip. Dee Dee fell like a stone. Coach Charles filled the air with colorful language, then barked at Matt to get on the field.

Matt's mind raced as he headed toward the huddle. This is my big chance, he thought. The Panthers! If I do well here, I could become starting quarterback.

Suddenly Matt's heart skipped a beat. But ... what if I fail?

Blind choice:

Without looking ahead, turn to page 34 or page 37 to continue the story.

Available NOW!!!

You'll want to read more sensational **What Would You Do?** novels ... filled with new characters, more spine-tingling decisions and loads of thrilling endings. Don't miss these new **What Would You Do?** books ...

He Gave Her Roses *By Vicki Grove*
You'll make the decisions for Stacy as she faces the uncertain world of dating and sexual pressures.
ISBN 0-931529-92-1 $6.95

Just This Once *By Dean Feldmeyer*
Help David make choices to avoid the lure of drugs and alcohol.
ISBN 1-55945-106-8 $6.95

A Time to Belong *By Vicki Grove*
You'll meet Ann, a Christian teenager, who faces everyday choices to make and keep friends and withstand negative peer pressure.
ISBN 1-55945-051-7 $6.95

These **What Would You Do?** books are available from your local Christian bookstore. For more information, or to order direct from the publisher, contact Teenage Books, Box 481, Loveland, CO 80539.